STRENGTHSQUEST:

DISCOVER AND DEVELOP YOUR STRENGTHS IN ACADEMICS, CAREER, AND BEYOND

Donald O. Clifton, Ph.D. &
Edward "Chip" Anderson, Ph.D.

THE GALLUP ORGANIZATION

Washington, D.C.

The Gallup Organization
Gallup, Inc.
901 F Street, NW
Washington, D.C. 20004

Cover design by Christopher Purdy
Manufactured in the United States of America

First edition 2002

10 9 8 7 6 5 4 3 2 1

ISBN 0-9722637-0-5

to those who helped me discover my strengths:
my wife Shirley, and our family
—DON

to God, my Creator, who inspired this work, gave me talents to do this
work, and guided me to my beloved wife, Irma
—CHIP

Table of Contents

STRENGTHSQUEST:

DISCOVER AND DEVELOP YOUR STRENGTHS IN ACADEMICS, CAREER, AND BEYOND

Preface

I was wrong!

For nearly half of my professional career, I was wrong about how to help students achieve. I had the wrong focus, made inaccurate assumptions, used faulty logic, and came to the wrong conclusions about how to increase student achievement.

During almost 36 years as a college administrator and instructor, I designed programs and services, taught classes, and conducted workshops with one purpose in mind: Help students gain maximum benefits from college and continue achieving long after they are done with school.

But looking back, I now see that for the first 15 years, despite my best intentions, I was using the wrong approach. About the only thing I did right during those early years was to invest myself in students, express my care and concern for them as people, and encourage them. But although a high percentage of my students persisted in and graduated from the programs in which I worked, they seldom became top achievers, and few achieved to levels of excellence.

Here is where and how I went wrong: I had read the research reports that clearly indicated a correlation between academic preparation and achievement. Results from almost every study on students in high school and college showed a direct correlation between students' levels of academic preparation and their subsequent achievement and persistence in college. The statistics showed that students who had the best academic preparation earned the highest grades and persisted to graduation in larger numbers. Students who had the weakest academic preparation earned the lowest grades and had the lowest graduation rates.

Armed with this information, I began designing procedures to identify the students who were least prepared so that we could build programs and services that would help more students achieve. I assumed that there were certain preparation levels that students needed in order to achieve; that if students met or exceeded these preparation levels, everything would take care of itself; that if students were prepared and met the expectations of the professors, then the normal courses of study and interactions with faculty would be sufficient to help students develop and achieve.

But I began to see two potential problems with my assumptions.

1. Many students don't have the expected level of preparation.

2. The whole issue of preparation is complex, because there are many types of preparation that students require in order to achieve.

After interviewing hundreds of students who were dropping out, experiencing difficulties, or flunking out of college, I came to believe that the types of preparation students needed included three broad areas: academic skills, background knowledge, and self-management skills. Within each of these areas, there were several specific types of skills and knowledge that instructors expected.

Assuming that certain skills and knowledge were essential to student success, I organized various diagnostic, testing, and assessment procedures to determine the extent to which each student was prepared in various areas. Diagnostic and assessment areas included reading speed and comprehension, vocabulary level, knowledge of mathematical concepts and problem solving, knowledge of grammar and writing skills, knowledge and problem solving in chemistry and physics, knowledge of study skills and study attitudes, and time and stress management. Using a combination of standardized tests, institutionally developed instruments, and interview procedures, I tried to get a clear picture of whether each student was prepared or underprepared.

In fact, I was very much influenced by the Deficit Remediation Educational Model, which has been predominant in education for decades. This model assumes that the first and most important thing to do is to "fix" the student. Programs and services based on this model are dedicated to helping students achieve by first diagnosing student needs, problems, ignorance, concerns, defects, and deficits. Those who use the Deficit Remediation Educational Model have the challenge of designing classes, workshops, programs, and services to help students improve in areas where they are underprepared. Based on the diagnosis, participation in remedial programs and services is often required. Students are usually prevented from pursuing other areas of study and from pursuing their interests until their "deficits" have been removed and their "problems" have been overcome.

Using this approach, students are usually told that they must overcome their deficiencies by a specific time. If they are unable to overcome their deficiencies by the established date, students are usually dismissed or told that they aren't "college material."

Mea culpa. I designed and implemented educational programs and services based on this model for almost 15 years, with the best of intentions. In retrospect, it is crystal clear that I was actually preventing students from becoming top achievers.

The Conference That Changed My Life

In the winter of 1978, I attended a conference on college student retention, sponsored by American College Testing (ACT), which brought together some of the best researchers and practitioners in this field. The conference coordinators were Drs. Lee Noel and Randi Levitz, who later founded the largest consulting organization in college student recruitment and retention, Noel-Levitz Inc.

Drs. Noel and Levitz gave presentations on why nearly half of the students who go to college drop out or flunk out along the way. They presented research findings and described some of the most effective programs and services designed to help more students persist to graduation. Another presenter at this conference was Dr. Robert Cope, coauthor of the book *Revolving College Doors*. He presented the best theory and research available about the causes of student persistence and attrition.

From the combination of presentations by Drs. Noel, Levitz, and Cope, I was forced to come to a radically new conclusion about college-student success:

> More students leave college because of disillusionment, discouragement, or reduced motivation than because of lack of ability or dismissal by school administration.

It is difficult to describe how mind boggling this new conclusion was for me. I discovered that I had been wrong in my logic and wrong in the way I designed programs and services. Before the conference, I had concluded that students were leaving college because they lacked certain skills, knowledge, and abilities. All the work I had done was based on this premise.

With the dawning awareness that I had been operating from the wrong perspective, I was eventually forced to an even more devastating conclusion:

> The deficit-based, remediation programming I had used for more than 10 years *interfered* with students becoming top achievers.

As I make these confessions, I feel bad about what I did unwittingly. I hindered students from achieving to levels of excellence.

But I wasn't alone. The deficit-based remediation approach was widely embraced by educators — and, unfortunately, remains the most prevalent approach used today. While most educators claim to identify not only the weaknesses but also the talents and strengths of their students, in practice, most focus almost solely on the weaknesses. Many students become demoralized and disillusioned.

The Impact of Meeting Donald O. Clifton

At the same conference in San Francisco, I met the man I feel so honored to know and write this book with: my coauthor, Dr. Donald O. Clifton. Don was introduced as a former professor at the University of Nebraska who had been voted Most Outstanding Educator for the state of Nebraska. Don had gone on to form a company called Selection Research, Incorporated, which helped companies do a better job of selecting employees through studying the "best of the best" in particular roles and positions. He eventually became chairman of The Gallup Organization, the global management consulting, training, and polling company.

I will never forget how Don slowly walked to the front of the stage, turned to the audience, and quickly had us riveted. His presentation drove home a significant point:

To produce excellence, you must study excellence.

Don's point hit me hard. Once again, I was wrong! In my efforts to help students persist and achieve, I had been studying dropouts. I should have been studying excellence. But back then, it seemed reasonable that to increase student persistence, I needed to study why students were leaving school and flunking out. Likewise, it seemed reasonable that to improve student achievement, I needed to study why people didn't achieve. Therefore, I spent endless hours interviewing dropouts and students who were underachieving.

It never occurred to me that I might be studying the wrong students to produce the best insights on how to help students achieve to levels of excellence. When I returned to UCLA after the conference in San Francisco, I began reading and trying to understand what made top achievers tick. Time and time again, I found that I had made inaccurate assumptions about the differences between top achievers and low achievers.

For example, I had always assumed that top achievers set high goals, and low achievers set low goals. But research indicates that top achievers tend to set goals slightly above their current level of performance, whereas low achievers often set very, very high goals.

The combination of reading books and articles, sitting in on classes, attending workshops, and consulting with scholars in the field reinforced Don's contention that if you want to produce excellence, you have to study excellence.

Here is the most important insight I have gained from investigating excellence among college students: Top achievers aren't all alike. There are huge variations in how they approach learning and studying. Some seem to learn best in isolation, while others learn best in social settings. Some learn best through group discussions, while others learn best from self-testing and repetition. There isn't any "one size fits all" set of learning and study techniques. Top achievers capitalize on their own personal uniqueness as they learn.

Essentially, top achievers build their academic and personal lives — and later their careers — on their talents. They develop talents into strengths and apply those strengths, and they manage their weaknesses. This strengths-based approach is the same approach that Don Clifton has always advocated, and its effectiveness is supported by decades of research by Gallup, where Don now serves as chairman of the Gallup International Research & Education Center.

This book and the strengths-based approach to achieving in academics, career, and beyond represent a revolutionary departure from traditional and counterproductive philosophies and practices. We hope that its principles resonate with you, and that you apply the strengths-based approach to achieving success in all of your life's endeavors!

—Edward "Chip" Anderson

Chapter I

THE NATURE OF STRENGTHS

IMPORTANT

Your ID code is located on the front inside cover of this book. Before you begin to read this book, it is essential that you use your ID code to log on to the StrengthsQuest Web site and take the StrengthsFinder assessment.

Go to:

http://student.strengthsquest.com

Minimum system requirements for the StrengthsQuest Web site:
- 33.6K modem (56K modem or faster recommended)
- Internet Explorer 5.0 or Netscape Navigator 6.0

Begin the StrengthsQuest program by taking StrengthsFinder.

StrengthsFinder is a 30-minute, Web-based assessment that measures the presence of 34 themes of talent. Immediately after you complete the assessment, a personalized Web site will be built around your top five themes. Taking StrengthsFinder is a key starting point for your use of this book and the other StrengthsQuest components, including:

- A personalized version of this book, which will feature insights and strategies customized to your Signature Themes. You'll be able to download and print full and condensed versions of the personalized book.

- The StrengthsQuest Learning Center, which will give you the opportunity to explore each of the 34 themes in an interactive learning format and test your knowledge of each theme. You'll also be able to create a personalized action plan based on your Signature Themes.

- The Online Strengths Community, which will enable you to communicate with other StrengthsQuest users and will provide you with additional strengths-based resources.

To purchase additional ID codes for the
StrengthsQuest program, please visit
http://www.strengthsquest.com

At the 1996 Olympic Games in Atlanta, Kerri Strug was a gymnast on the United States women's gold medal team. Her performance on the vault, as she nursed an injured ankle, remains one of the most memorable in Olympic history.

With 32,000 people in the Georgia Dome and millions watching her on television, Kerri fell on her first attempt at her most difficult twisting vault, severely spraining her left ankle. With less than a minute between vaults, and in great pain, she again attempted the vault, further injuring her ankle — but this time successfully landing on both feet. So she stood erect on one foot, raising both hands to salute the judges, then collapsed to her knees.

The crowd went wild. Kerri's vault earned a 9.712, and the U.S. women won the gold medal.

During that same year, Kerri was a freshman at UCLA. One of her classes required a research paper similar to a mini-doctoral dissertation. Students had to formulate their own research question and develop a questionnaire that was consistent with their research question. Then, the students would administer the questionnaire, collect and analyze the data, draw conclusions, and write a report that described the process. The written report was to be 35-40 pages long.

Taking the StrengthsFinder assessment was one of the class requirements. When Kerri took it, she scored extremely high in the Focus theme. But doesn't that make sense? Who else but a person with tremendous Focus strengths could concentrate on completing her most difficult vault on an injured ankle in front of 32,000 screaming fans while Olympic gold hung in the balance? Who else could block out all of those distractions and then land on one foot without falling?

While Kerri certainly had other strengths that enabled her to succeed, her Focus strengths played a critical role. Without them, she might never have enjoyed such stunning Olympic success.

But there's more to the story. Toward the end of the fall term, as research papers were coming due, Kerri turned her paper in three days early, before any of the other 300-plus UCLA students in the class. She did this while traveling nearly every weekend on a national tour with fellow Olympic medallists. Even more remarkable was the way that Kerri could go out on an arena floor, do a routine, and then go underneath the stands and work on the paper. She would then go back out on the floor and do another routine and return to do more homework.

You see, Kerri also applied her Focus strengths to succeed in academics.

Kerri is a remarkable young woman. But the excellence she achieved wasn't due simply to the fact that she naturally possessed talents. She recognized her Focus talents and developed them to a point of strength — the point at which those talents were incredibly powerful and enabled her to produce consistent, near-perfect performance. She obviously did so at the Olympics — even while in severe pain and under tremendous pressure — but she was also able to apply her Focus in academics, where she achieved despite rigorous assignments and the myriad pressures of her athletic career.

Kerri has presented each of us with more than a shared pride in her Olympic success. We can learn from her. You, too, have talents. And in those talents you have the ability to meet challenges and achieve just as surely as Kerri did.

The Basics of Strengths

Talent: The Beginning of Strength

What is a strength? That's a good question, but a strength begins with a talent, so let's start there. A talent is a naturally recurring pattern of thought, feeling, or behavior that can be productively applied. A great number of talents naturally exist within you, and each of them is very specific. They are among the most real and most authentic aspects of your personhood. Your specific set of talents is a major part of what makes you a unique person, and that uniqueness holds great value for you and those around you. And your talents work in various combinations each time you do something very well, in your own unique way.

There is a direct connection between your talents and your achievements. Your talents empower you. They make it possible for you to move to higher levels of excellence and fulfill your potential. This is why it is so important for you to know, understand, and value your talents.

A talent represents a capacity to *do* something. In fact, when you are able to do something very well, you can be sure that at least one of your talents is involved. Just think about all the things you do very well. You'll realize that you have many talents!

And not only do talents help you do something well once, they help you do it well over and over again. Because talents are naturally recurring patterns, they are "automatic," almost like breathing, so they repeatedly help you achieve.

That's not all, either. Each of your many talents can enable you to do more than one thing very well. We're not saying that each of your talents enables you to do *everything* very well, but know that each of your talents can be applied to multiple areas of achievement.

The great value in your talents is not merely that they help you achieve, but that they help you achieve at levels of *excellence*. Your greatest talents are inextricably linked to your top achievements and to what you do best. Your talents make you exceptional. Therefore, coming to know, understand, and value your talents is directly linked to achieving in classes, careers, and throughout your life.

Talent Versus Other Concepts of Ability

The concept of talent is more specific in terms of the quality it describes and the things that various types of talent help a person to do very well. Traditional concepts and measures of ability (for example, I.Q. and aptitude testing) are more global and are not designed to explain what a person can specifically do.

The concept of talent goes beyond the limits of traditional concepts of academic abilities (for example, in the areas of reading, math, and composition) in that it also addresses the qualities that help a person achieve in all aspects of life.

The 34 Themes of Talent Measured by StrengthsFinder

What is a theme? Essentially, a theme is a group of similar talents. Kerri Strug once again provides a good illustration. Kerri used a wide variety of talents in the Focus theme to achieve in athletics and academics. Among them was her talent for focusing on the precise steps required to perform complicated gymnastic maneuvers, and, during the intense pressure of the Olympics, her talent for blocking out the distraction of intense pain to produce a gold-medal performance.

Kerri used other types of talents, too. Her talents in the Adaptability theme enabled her to achieve excellence in athletics and academics at the same time. Her talent to balance two extremely high priorities, easily moving from one to the other, was crucial to her success in each area.

As a result of studying top achievers for more than three decades, The Gallup Organization was able to identify more than 400 different themes of talent. The 34 most prevalent themes are measured by StrengthsFinder.

Back to Your Question: What Is a Strength?

Now, let's go to the definition of a strength: A strength is the ability to provide consistent, near-perfect performance in a given activity.

As you read earlier, the concept of strengths begins with talent. Each person naturally has a group of talents. Talents are like "diamonds in the rough," whereas strengths are like diamonds that show brilliance after they have been carefully cut and polished.

Your greatest areas of talent, your most likely sources of potential strengths, are identified by StrengthsFinder.

Just as finished diamonds start as diamonds in the rough, strengths start as talents. And just as rough diamonds are naturally found in the earth, talents are naturally found within you. But while diamonds are refined with blades and polishing wheels, strengths are produced when talents are refined with *knowledge* and *skill*.

Unlike talent, which must naturally exist within you, skills and knowledge can be acquired. Skills are the ability to perform the specific steps of an activity. Knowledge consists of facts and lessons learned.

Many of the skills and much of the knowledge used to refine a talent into a strength come through experience, and sometimes a great deal of it. Skills and knowledge are also developed in a "book learning" sense, such as in the academic arenas of high school, college, technical school, and training classes.

When you have refined a talent to the point at which you can provide consistent, near-perfect performance in a given activity, you have a strength. And in applying and even further developing your strengths, you move closer and closer to fulfilling your natural potential as an individual.

Each person has a unique and profound set and combination of talents and strengths that are developed and used to different degrees. This combination of talents and strengths makes each person like no other.

While each person defines success for himself or herself, achievement and excellence result from fully developing and applying strengths. Some roles require several strengths, all working together, to produce excellence. You probably have already developed some strengths, and you certainly will have plenty of opportunity to develop more strengths throughout your lifetime.

What Do Strengths Produce?

As you develop and use strengths, achievements will naturally follow. But there is also a great sense of personal satisfaction that results from knowing that you are becoming more and more of whom you have the potential to be. In a sense, the development and application of strengths generate a feeling that you are fulfilling your personal destiny. This can produce enormous satisfaction and enhance the quality of your life.

While the experiences of individual people differ tremendously, most report that it is a rewarding experience to be fully living in tune with their natural talents by building and using strengths. Almost everyone reports increased confidence and optimism as they become aware of, affirm, and celebrate their talents. Many report "coming alive," or even feeling joy as they develop and apply strengths. Reports about the exact inner experiences may differ, but nearly everyone who develops and uses strengths reports a sense of positive and pleasant psychological rewards.

Our initial goal is for you to become more aware of your talents and your potential strengths. We hope you are filled with appreciation for your particular talents, for the positive differences they have already made in your life, and for the excellence strengths can produce in your future achievements, relationships, and other life experiences.

The Beauty of Strengths: Angel Alcoser

Angel Alcoser is an extraordinarily talented educator. She stands in front of her bilingual kindergarten/first-grade class and performs her role with poise, grace, and excellence — yet with no formal training.

Angel obtained an "emergency credential" to teach the year she graduated from college. She hadn't taken any courses in curriculum design, teaching methods, or assessment. But somehow she knew what to do and did it as if she were a magician generating one creative learning activity after another.

At the beginning of one class, which two visitors were observing, Angel stood before the children and said, "Boys and girls, would you like to perform for our guests?"

With a rousing "Yes," the children lined up.

As Angel walked over to the tape recorder on a table by the wall, every eye was on her. She pushed the "play" button, and with the first note, the

children burst into a breathtaking show of song and dance. The visitors were moved, even spellbound.

Angel later explained how she prepared to do her work as an educator. She related a story about the children and the potential she saw in each one of them and how she tried to involve parents and make her classroom like a family. Then, she talked about how important it was to connect with every child, emphasizing the importance of seeing each one as a unique person.

"Most of the children in my class come from very humble homes," Angel said. "Some are neglected; some are abused. But," she asserted, "I can't control much of what goes on outside of my class. I do what I can! Once they are in my class, they are all safe. In my class, they can grow to be more than they have ever been."

Angel continued, "I don't focus on what they don't have. I focus on who they are and what they have to offer. I challenge the students to see what they do have, not what they don't. I want them to see that each of them has something that makes them special. They are each talented in some way. Some of the children are great storytellers; others seem to be natural leaders; still others are wonderful organizers. Regardless of the type of talent, I start with the child and what each of them can do best."

How does Angel recognize the children's talents?

"I listen. I look. I see them. I work at it every day! Almost every day, I stay after class. I sit in the classroom and meditate about each child. I let my imagination go and imagine each child both in terms of who they are now and the person they can become."

Angel spoke glowingly about one young lady in her class, who often wore a little blue cap that flopped over her ears. The girl, Delia, carried an old file folder with accordion sides. "She's from a very humble home," Angel said. "It's only her and her mother, who sells oranges on street corners. They are very poor. But Delia has a dream that one day she will become a doctor. Every day, she picks up papers and stuffs them in her little folder. She does this because she pretends that she is already in college and that those papers are the homework assignments for her college classes."

At the end of the school year, Angel presided over the children's graduation ceremony. Each child was encouraged to invite one or more family members, and this really excited the children. More than 30 people attended. The children performed as a group with dance and music, singing

alternately in English and Spanish.

The formal graduation ceremony began with the children taking their little chairs and making a large circle in the middle of the room. Angel stepped into the middle of the circle carrying a large box. Then, she called each child's name one by one, and each child went up to the box and pulled out a picture frame containing a piece of paper with printing and handwriting, a picture in the middle, and brightly colored stars around the border.

As the children got their framed pieces of paper, they turned and walked back to their chairs and handed their framed works of art to the parents and other guests they had invited.

At the conclusion of the ceremony, Angel read what was on the framed pieces of paper:

"I was born to dream big dreams. I would like to be _____ when I grow up."

In the blank space, each child wrote his or her goal, the career they hoped to enter. Then, there was the picture of the child. In bold print beneath the child's picture were these words: "Yes, I can do it. Give me your unconditional love and tell me every day that I was born to do beautiful things. With much love." And then there was a line where each child wrote his or her name.

The Best of the Best All Have One Thing in Common

Angel Alcoser, in both her excellence in teaching and her approach to students, exemplifies what The Gallup Organization has discovered through more than two million in-depth interviews with people from all walks of life: Top achievers in virtually every profession, career, and field of achievement all build their lives upon their talents.

This simple but profound finding forms the heart of this book. You see, Angel isn't one of the "best of the best" by accident. She has achieved excellence because she has capitalized on her talents. In fact, she has built her teaching strategies, even her whole life, on her talents.

Findings From Gallup's Study of the Best

Here is what Gallup knows about top achievers.

Top achievers fully recognize their talents and develop them into

strengths. In contrast, underachievers, the merely average, and even above-average achievers often fail to recognize their talents and develop them into strengths. But the best achievers are certain to do so.

Top achievers apply their strengths in roles that best suit them. Clearly, to achieve, one must apply his or her abilities, and many do so to some level of success. But the best apply their strengths and do so in roles that are best suited to those strengths. The ability to achieve with excellence in one area is not proof of the ability to perform equally well in another area. A proper "fit" between an individual's strengths and the task at hand is essential.

Top achievers invent ways to apply their strengths to their achievement tasks. Every role, position, and career entails a group of tasks that must be completed, and quite often the person who performs them must consciously seek, even invent, ways to apply his or her strengths to that end — even when one's role is well suited to his or her strengths.

How Angel Alcoser Uses Three of Her Signature Themes

Angel took the StrengthsFinder assessment, which identifies your top five themes of talent — your Signature Themes. In both her role as an educator and her personal life, she primarily uses strengths that she has developed from talents in three of her Signature Themes.

1. Maximizer: People strong in the Maximizer theme focus on strengths as a way to stimulate personal and group excellence. They seek to transform something strong into something superb.

2. Connectedness: People strong in the Connectedness theme have faith in the links between all things. They believe there are few coincidences and that almost every event has a reason.

3. Developer: People strong in the Developer theme recognize and cultivate the potential in others. They spot the signs of each small improvement and derive satisfaction from these improvements.

You can easily see how Angel used Maximizer and Developer strengths as she worked with the children. Remember that she said that she focused on who the children were, rather than who they weren't. Angel started out with the assumption that each child had "some talent, some strength."

Angel's ability to perceive talent in the children, her ability to notice progress, and her ability to mirror what she sees in each child are not coincidences. Angel has an abundance of strengths within the Developer and Maximizer themes.

Angel's Connectedness strengths are reflected in her determination to connect with children and their families. Connectedness also comes into play as she sets up her classroom with a family atmosphere.

Mostly, Angel's Connectedness strengths are revealed in the way she meditates after school and envisions each child. She is looking for talents within each child and for the role she can play in their development. Her Connectedness strengths enable her to see a bigger picture, a bigger plan.

What makes Angel Alcoser such an outstanding educator starts with who she is as a person. Her natural talents are the source of her excellence. She is simply being her true self. Understand this: Top achievers fully develop whatever talents they happen to possess and apply the resulting strengths in a way that positively impacts their role or the task at hand.

The Tragedy of Undiscovered Talents

Less than five miles from where Angel first taught, there is another elementary school. A young girl by the name of Leonor was a student there in the 1950s. When Leonor was 10 years old, she and her parents emigrated to the United States from Mexico. She had done very well in school in in her native country, but she didn't know any English, so classes in the United States would be much more difficult for her. Nevertheless, she was anxious to go to school, because it had always been a positive experience for her in Mexico.

In fact, Leonor had always had a secret desire to become a teacher. She had two great aunts who were teachers, and she greatly admired them.

Because she could neither read nor write in English, Leonor was held back and repeated the fourth grade. Her fourth-grade teacher volunteered to stay after school to help her learn English. Leonor worked hard throughout elementary, junior high, and high school. In her sophomore, junior, and senior years of high school, Leonor earned almost straight A's, and each year she was on the honor roll and in the Honors Society. She graduated near the top of her class.

Unfortunately, Leonor never had a teacher like Angel, who could lead her to discover her natural talents. And despite the fact that she was an honor student, no one ever asked if she might be interested in attending college.

The year Leonor graduated from high school, her father lost his job. So, Leonor got a job in a business close to her home and would turn her paycheck over to her parents so they could pay the rent and buy food for the whole family.

For the next 33 years, Leonor worked in the banking industry and hated almost every day that she went to work. What's sad — even tragic — is that Leonor was convinced that she had no talents.

The tragedy for Leonor wasn't in where she worked or what she did. Banking is a fine and respectable profession, and Leonor advanced to vice president and administrative manager of a branch office. Clearly, Leonor achieved, and her 33 years in banking were not a squandering of time. However, those years could have been immensely more fulfilling if Leonor had been aware of her natural talents. Fortunately, over the last three years, Leonor has gone through the process of discovering the talents she has had from the beginning, developing them into strengths, and applying those strengths. Following her talents, Leonor has transitioned from banking into teaching, where she is experiencing joy and excitement like she never has before.

Your Strengths Quest Begins With You

As described earlier, the seeds of your personal greatness — your talents — are already in you. Therefore, your strengths quest — your quest to achieve excellence and become all you can be through your own natural talents — is really a quest to discover, develop, and apply who you truly are. Your strengths quest begins as you look within yourself as an individual to recognize your own natural talents.

Your strengths quest will then continue as you develop your talents into strengths — abilities to provide consistent, near-perfect performances in specific activities. As you do this, your self-identity and personal values should become clearer, and as a result, you will likely become more confident, optimistic, and focused. As you achieve through your strengths, you will likely aspire to higher goals.

Your strengths quest is a lifelong adventure. Each of the three aspects

— discovery, development, and application — will continue throughout your life. This exciting and fulfilling process should bring you a lifetime of great satisfaction and joy.

Chapter II

GAINING DIRECTION FOR YOUR QUEST

A strengths quest is a revolutionary approach to achieving. Why? Because adopting a strengths perspective to your life and fully embracing it has a radical impact on your motivation. Your awareness, development, and application of your strengths are inextricably linked to your motivation level. To the extent that you fully involve yourself in a strengths quest, your motivation will increase, and that will revolutionize your life.

Your Strengths Quest and Your Motivations

So, what exactly are the connections between your strengths quest and your motivations?

1. **Your quest addresses your questions.**
   Most great scholars know that motivation to conduct research, and to learn in general, stems from personally meaningful questions to which they want to find answers.

2. **Your quest is an adventure of discovery.**
   A quest is motivating simply because of the adventure and the discoveries you will make along the way. The first adventure is discovering your talents — but that is only the beginning. Then, there are discoveries and insights that will come to you as you gain a strengths perspective on your entire life. Suddenly, you will begin to understand the connection between your talents and your past achievements.

3. **Your quest generates optimism.**
   As you become increasingly aware of your talents, you will become more optimistic, because you realize that you have abilities you can use in pursuing your goals. This alone builds motivation because you recognize that in your talents, you in fact have assets that can help you reach your desired goals.

4. **Your quest provides a sense of direction.**
   Being lost is a dreadful experience. One of the most motivating aspects of a strengths quest is the increased sense of direction that comes as you gain a greater understanding of who you are.

5. **Your quest generates confidence.**

As you become more and more aware of your talents and as you develop them into strengths, you will become more aware of your potential for excellence. As a result, you will gain confidence.

6. **Your quest generates a sense of vitality.**

Whenever you use your strengths, there is a psychological reward — you receive both satisfaction and motivation. The pleasurable experience of using your strengths seems to reach some of your deepest motivations. When you are using your strengths, you seem to become more fully alive.

Your Signature Themes Report

Let's turn now to your Signature Themes report, which you received after completing the StrengthsFinder assessment.

As described earlier, your Signature Themes are your five most dominant themes of talent, as indicated by your responses to the assessment. They are presented in rank order, with your most dominant theme listed first. Each Signature Theme is accompanied by a description of that theme.

Some people are concerned about receiving only their top five themes. That's understandable, but Gallup research clearly points to the fact that the top achievers focus on their most dominant areas of talent, and we would like you to do the same. Attempting to focus on too many themes can dilute the attention you give to your top themes. Also, we don't want you to fall prey to the conventional "wisdom" that the best way to achieve is to focus on your areas of lesser talent. We want you to focus on your Signature Themes — your greatest areas of talent — which present your best opportunities to achieve.

What Should You Do With Your Signature Themes Report?

The rest of this book is devoted to answering this question. But there are two things that we would like you to do as soon as possible.

First, please print a copy of your report, and carefully read the descriptions of each of your Signature Themes. Please underline or highlight each term, phrase, and sentence that seems to describe you.

Next, contact the three people who know you best, and read each of your Signature Themes and their descriptions. After reading each description, please ask these people if they see that Signature Theme in you. If they say yes, ask them to give you an example of when they have seen it in you. If any of them answer no, simply move on to the next Signature Theme.

You are a talented person with a unique and very special set of talents. Now, it's time to learn more about them and gain further direction for your strengths quest by affirming your Signature Themes.

Chapter III

AFFIRMING AND CELEBRATING YOUR TALENTS

You have taken StrengthsFinder, received your Signature Themes report, and discussed your Signature Themes with three people who know you very well. Now, it's time for you to affirm the Signature Themes indicated by your StrengthsFinder responses.

Affirming a Signature Theme simply means that you *agree* that it is one of your dominant areas of talent. It also means being able to see how your talent in that theme enables you to do certain things very well. Affirming your Signature Themes may seem easy, but many people experience some difficulty in doing so. Listed below are some of those difficulties and the reasons for them.

Difficulties in Affirming Our Signature Themes

1. Many people are blind to their own greatest talents, and often to the greatest talents of others. Some of our talents are called upon so frequently that we take them for granted. We don't consider them special, and we don't even perceive them as talents. Consequently, our Signature Themes may not seem important, valuable, or even special to us.

2. Our talents sometimes threaten others. Rather than admit their insecurity, some people criticize us for having talents they wish they had. As a result, we might mistakenly come to think that our Signature Themes hold weaknesses rather than talents.

3. In some cases, we end up in positions or roles that simply don't fit our dominant talents. Or, those talents may conflict with the roles and expectations of the positions we are in. This can make us feel like there is something wrong with us. But the problem may only be a mismatch between our dominant talents and the expectations of a role we are in.

4. The fear of becoming proud and arrogant may interfere with seeing and affirming our Signature Themes. In reality, pride and arrogance often stem from feelings of inadequacy. Affirming our dominant areas of talent usually results in humble gratitude for having been blessed with them.

5. Some people have difficulty affirming their Signature Themes because they don't see how the talents in them will help them

achieve their goals. If that is the case, they will benefit from a better understanding of their talents. Talents are always valuable, and they can often be applied toward achievement in less obvious, or even surprising, ways.

Questions You Might Be Asking

If a Particular Theme Is Not Among Your Signature Themes, Is It Necessarily an Area of Weakness?

No. StrengthsFinder *does not* simultaneously measure weakness and talent. StrengthsFinder measures talent, and that's all it does. So, if a particular theme is not among your Signature Themes, it simply means that at least five other themes are more dominant in you.

For example, your Responsibility theme might not be among your Signature Themes. That doesn't mean you are irresponsible. It just means that your overall talents in at least five other themes are more dominant than those in your Responsibility theme.

By focusing on your Signature Themes, you will concentrate your attention on where you have the greatest potential for achieving excellence and personal fulfillment. Focusing on any other area may serve as nothing more than a distraction.

What If You Believe You Have Dominant Talent in a Theme That Was Not Identified as a Signature Theme?

Our response is simple and direct: Claim it! Affirm and celebrate the fact that you have it, then fully develop and apply strengths in that theme. Just remember that we limited your Signature Themes to five because focusing on your *most* dominant areas of talent will provide the greatest opportunities for achievement.

Is Having Talent Always a Positive Experience?

Talent is always positive in the sense that it enables a person to do certain things very well. Your talents always hold potential for positive results in terms of achievements, success, personal fulfillment, and a better quality of life.

At the same time, talents place demands on the people who have them. And from that standpoint, talents can present a bit of a challenge.

Some people honestly say that they wish that their talents weren't so strong in certain themes because they make their lives more demanding. They simply may experience more pressure because other people place higher expectations on them to achieve.

Affirming Your Signature Themes

Affirming Your Signature Themes While Acknowledging Challenges They May Pose

On your Signature Themes report, each of your Signature Themes is accompanied by a paragraph that describes talents often found within that theme. While some of the talents described may not fit you, many of the talents described should sound very familiar — and that is what is important. The issue is not who you *aren't*; the issue is who you *are* in terms of your dominant talents.

At this point, we would like you to consider insights and action ideas for affirming your Signature Themes. Strategies for each of the 34 themes measured by StrengthsFinder are presented here, in alphabetical order by theme. Please locate and examine the strategies that are customized to your Signature Themes.

We hope that as you think about your Signature Themes, you reach two key conclusions. First, we hope you will see that within each of your Signature Themes, you possess many useful talents. Second, we hope that you recognize within those talents your natural potential for strength — and for the achievement of excellence.

Achiever as One of Your Signature Themes

To begin affirming Achiever as one of your dominant areas of talent, first take another look at the description of that theme:

Your Achiever theme helps explain your drive. Achiever describes a constant need for achievement. You feel as if every day starts at zero. By the end of the day you must achieve something tangible in order to feel good about yourself. And by "every day" you mean every single day — workdays, weekends, vacations. No matter how much you may feel you deserve a day of rest, if the day passes without some form of achievement, no matter how small, you will feel dissatisfied. You have an internal fire burning inside you. It pushes you to do more, to achieve more. After each accomplishment is reached, the fire dwindles for a moment, but very soon it rekindles itself, forcing you toward the next accomplishment. Your relentless need for achievement might not be logical. It might not even be focused. But it will always be with you. As an Achiever you must learn to live with this whisper of discontent. It does have its benefits. It brings you the energy you need to work long hours without burning out. It is the jolt you can always count on to get you started on new tasks, new challenges. It is the power supply that causes you to set the pace and define the levels of productivity for your work group. It is the theme that keeps you moving.

Now, consider this statement based on comments from individuals who possess Achiever among their Signature Themes. It represents what Achiever could "sound like."

"I'm going to earn an A in every class — and I'm going to ask my teachers for opportunities to earn extra credit so I can turn that A into an A+."

For further understanding of your talents, examine these five insights and select those that describe you best.

☐ You work very hard to complete each task on your "to do" list, and you always have a long list of things to do.

☐ You are busy, productive, and derive satisfaction from your accomplishments.

☐ You have a great deal of stamina and determination to achieve your goals.

☐ Other people may criticize you, because to them you seem too driven to achieve. They may call you a "workaholic" but the truth is that you like your work, and you like to work hard.

☐ Achiever talents are valuable because they help you remain motivated to reach your goals and to push for higher and higher levels of excellence. You won't rest until you reach your most highly desired goals — and they must be *your* goals.

Activator as One of Your Signature Themes

To begin affirming Activator as one of your dominant areas of talent, first take another look at the description of that theme:

"When can we start?" This is a recurring question in your life. You are impatient for action. You may concede that analysis has its uses or that debate and discussion can occasionally yield some valuable insights, but deep down you know that only action is real. Only action can make things happen. Only action leads to performance. Once a decision is made, you cannot not act. Others may worry that "there are still some things we don't know," but this doesn't seem to slow you. If the decision has been made to go across town, you know that the fastest way to get there is to go stoplight to stoplight. You are not going to sit around waiting until all the lights have turned green. Besides, in your view, action and thinking are not opposites. In fact, guided by your Activator theme, you believe that action is the best device for learning. You make a decision, you take action, you look at the result, and you learn. This learning informs your next action and your next. How can you grow if you have nothing to react to? Well, you believe you can't. You must put yourself out there. You must take the next step. It is the only way to keep your thinking fresh and informed. The bottom line is this: You know you will be judged not by what you say, not by what you think, but by what you get done. This does not frighten you. It pleases you.

Now, consider this statement based on comments from individuals who possess Activator among their Signature Themes. It represents what Activator could "sound like."

"I took over a project that was comatose. Things just weren't getting done -- nothing was moving. I decided to pull together a team and address key issues. We immediately made tremendous strides and are continuing to charge ahead."

For further understanding of your talents, examine these five insights and select those that describe you best.

☐ You can see how ideas can be turned into action.

☐ You want to do things now, rather than simply talk about doing them.

☐ You can be very powerful in making things happen and getting people to take action.

☐ Other people may criticize you for being impatient and seeming to "run over" them. You will probably struggle with people who try to control you.

☐ Activator talents are valuable because they generate the energy to get things going and then done. This theme brings innovation and creative approaches to problem solving.

Adaptability as One of Your Signature Themes

To begin affirming Adaptability as one of your dominant areas of talent, first take another look at the description of that theme:

You live in the moment. You don't see the future as a fixed destination. Instead, you see it as a place that you create out of the choices that you make right now. And so you discover your future one choice at a time. This doesn't mean that you don't have plans. You probably do. But this theme of Adaptability does enable you to respond willingly to the demands of the moment even if they pull you away from your plans. Unlike some, you don't resent sudden requests or unforeseen detours. You expect them. They are inevitable. Indeed, on some level you actually look forward to them. You are, at heart, a very flexible person who can stay productive when the demands of work are pulling you in many different directions at once.

Now, consider this statement based on comments from individuals who possess Adaptability among their Signature Themes. It represents what Adaptability could "sound like."

"I work in customer service. When I'm in the middle of helping a customer on the phone with a price check and another customer walks up to the counter for an exchange, I have to quickly adjust to an entirely different issue — and I'm good at it. It doesn't stress me; I enjoy going with the flow and taking care of both customers."

For further understanding of your talents, examine these five insights and select those that describe you best.

☐ You can modify yourself depending on the demands in your environment.

☐ You adjust to many things all day long because you live in the moment.

☐ You create and discover the future out of the choices you make right now, one choice at a time.

☐ Your "go with the flow" attitude may seem like irresponsibility to those who like structure and predictability.

☐ Adaptability talents are valuable because they allow you to keep moving forward when the unexpected happens. You can move ahead in a world of unknowns and seemingly unfair treatment when others would give up. You can deal with everything from injustices to crises and still find a way to make progress.

Analytical as One of Your Signature Themes

To begin affirming Analytical as one of your dominant areas of talent, first take another look at the description of that theme:

Your Analytical theme challenges other people: "Prove it. Show me why what you are claiming is true." In the face of this kind of questioning some will find that their brilliant theories wither and die. For you, this is precisely the point. You do not necessarily want to destroy other people's ideas, but you do insist that their theories be sound. You see yourself as objective and dispassionate. You like data because they are value free. They have no agenda. Armed with these data, you search for patterns and connections. You want to understand how certain patterns affect one another. How do they combine? What is their outcome? Does this outcome fit with the theory being offered or the situation being confronted? These are your questions. You peel the layers back until, gradually, the root cause or causes are revealed. Others see you as logical and rigorous. Over time they will come to you in order to expose someone's "wishful thinking" or "clumsy thinking" to your refining mind. It is hoped that your analysis is never delivered too harshly. Otherwise, others may avoid you when that "wishful thinking" is their own.

Now, consider this statement based on comments from individuals who possess Analytical among their Signature Themes. It represents what Analytical could "sound like."

"When I was a kid, I took a clock apart just to see how it worked. When I saw the gears and how they worked together, it made perfect sense. I was able put it back together very quickly."

For further understanding of your talents, examine these five insights and select those that describe you best.

☐ You search for the reasons why things are the way they are.

☐ You think about the factors that might affect a situation and what causes certain reactions.

☐ You are critical about why people may claim something is true and want to see the proof.

☐ Some people may reject you and your questioning ways because you insist that facts are verifiable, theories are sound, and reasoning is logical. Some people may think you are negative or unnecessarily critical when, from your standpoint, you are simply trying to understand something.

☐ Analytical talents are valuable because they enable you to dig deep, find the root causes and effects, and then develop clear thoughts about what is true. This type of thinking helps you become clearer about what excellence is and how it can be attained.

Arranger as One of Your Signature Themes

To begin affirming Arranger as one of your dominant areas of talent, first take another look at the description of that theme:

You are a conductor. When faced with a complex situation involving many factors, you enjoy managing all of the variables, aligning and re-aligning them until you are sure you have arranged them in the most productive configuration possible. In your mind there is nothing special about what you are doing. You are simply trying to figure out the best way to get things done. But others, lacking this theme, will be in awe of your ability. "How can you keep so many things in your head at once?" they will ask. "How can you stay so flexible, so willing to shelve well-laid plans in favor of some brand-new configuration that has just occurred to you?" But you cannot imagine behaving in any other way. You are a shining example of effective flexibility, whether you are changing travel schedules at the last minute because a better fare has popped up or mulling over just the right combination of people and resources to accomplish a new project. From the mundane to the complex, you are always looking for the perfect configuration. Of course, you are at your best in dynamic situations. Confronted with the unexpected, some complain that plans devised with such care cannot be changed, while others take refuge in the existing rules or procedures. You don't do either. Instead, you jump into the confusion, devising new options, hunting for new paths of least resistance, and figuring out new partnerships — because, after all, there might just be a better way.

Now, consider this statement based on comments from individuals who possess Arranger among their Signature Themes. It represents what Arranger could "sound like."

"The school year is wrapping up, which means that I have to study for finals and prepare to move out of the dorms, in addition to working my part-time job. Not a problem. I'll ask my boss to schedule me to work the days before my easier exams, which will give me more time to study for the tough ones. I'll pack during my study breaks."

For further understanding of your talents, examine these five insights and select those that describe you best.

☐ You are highly organized and highly flexible.

☐ You can get a lot done, even though you usually have many projects going at the same time.

☐ You enjoy coordinating all of the complex factors that go into making a project successful.

☐ Some people who like to do things by rules and procedures may find your ways chaotic. They may think that your effectiveness is mystery or pure luck.

☐ Arranger talents are valuable because they help you keep looking for the right combinations of people and resources to complete projects successfully.

Belief as One of Your Signature Themes

To begin affirming Belief as one of your dominant areas of talent, first take another look at the description of that theme:

If you possess a strong Belief theme, you have certain core values that are enduring. These values vary from one person to another, but ordinarily your Belief theme causes you to be family-oriented, altruistic, even spiritual, and to value responsibility and high ethics — both in yourself and others. These core values affect your behavior in many ways. They give your life meaning and satisfaction; in your view, success is more than money and prestige. They provide you with direction, guiding you through the temptations and distractions of life toward a consistent set of priorities. This consistency is the foundation for all your relationships. Your friends call you dependable. "I know where you stand," they say. Your Belief makes you easy to trust. It also demands that you find work that meshes with your values. Your work must be meaningful; it must matter to you. And guided by your Belief theme it will matter only if it gives you a chance to live out your values.

Now, consider this statement based on comments from individuals who possess Belief among their Signature Themes. It represents what Belief could "sound like."

"Obviously, my education is very important to me, so I have to devote a lot of time to my classes. But making a difference for the kids in my community is part of my personal mission. Regardless of my academic commitments, I make time to volunteer for the after-school program at the youth center."

For further understanding of your talents, examine these five insights and select those that describe you best.

☐ You have core values that are unchanging. You may conflict with people who oppose or don't value your beliefs.

☐ You have deeply held ideas about what is, what should be, and the purpose of your life.

☐ You will become energetic about a task, role, or position that promotes one of your deeply held beliefs.

☐ Some people may think you are rigid or contrary because of your strongly held beliefs.

☐ Belief talents are valuable because they produce the motivation for you to work hard, excel, and achieve, as long as achieving is consistent with your values and beliefs. Your set of beliefs does more than energize you — it is the basis for developing a meaningful life.

Command as One of Your Signature Themes

To begin affirming Command as one of your dominant areas of talent, first take another look at the description of that theme:

Command leads you to take charge. Unlike some people, you feel no discomfort with imposing your views on others. On the contrary, once your opinion is formed, you need to share it with others. Once your goal is set, you feel restless until you have aligned others with you. You are not frightened by confrontation; rather, you know that confrontation is the first step toward resolution. Whereas others may avoid facing up to life's unpleasantness, you feel compelled to present the facts or the truth, no matter how unpleasant it may be. You need things to be clear between people and challenge them to be clear-eyed and honest. You push them to take risks. You may even intimidate them. And while some may resent this, labeling you opinionated, they often willingly hand you the reins. People are drawn toward those who take a stance and ask them to move in a certain direction. Therefore, people will be drawn to you. You have presence. You have Command.

Now, consider this statement based on comments from individuals who possess Command among their Signature Themes. It represents what Command could "sound like."

"Some of my friends get nervous about making presentations in class, but I don't. When I'm in front of the class, people are going to listen to me, and I actually enjoy being in control."

For further understanding of your talents, examine these five insights and select those that describe you best.

☐ You see what needs to be done, and you are willing to say so.

☐ You are willing to go into a confrontation and argue because you know that what is right will prevail, and confrontations often help get things moving.

☐ You can jump into a conflict, crisis, or emergency and take charge of the situation.

☐ Other people may be threatened, offended, or put off by the power you can command, but most wish they had some of your talents.

☐ Command talents are valuable because they help you positively impact other people. You can help people and entire organizations get through difficult times and make substantive changes in the midst of chaos.

Communication as One of Your Signature Themes

To begin affirming Communication as one of your dominant areas of talent, first take another look at the description of that theme:

You like to explain, to describe, to host, to speak in public, and to write. This is your Communication theme at work. Ideas are a dry beginning. Events are static. You feel a need to bring them to life, to energize them, to make them exciting and vivid. And so you turn events into stories and practice telling them. You take the dry idea and enliven it with images and examples and metaphors. You believe that most people have a very short attention span. They are bombarded by information, but very little of it survives. You want your information — whether an idea, an event, a product's features and benefits, a discovery, or a lesson — to survive. You want to divert their attention toward you and then capture it, lock it in. This is what drives your hunt for the perfect phrase. This is what draws you toward dramatic words and powerful word combinations. This is why people like to listen to you. Your word pictures pique their interest, sharpen their world, and inspire them to act.

Now, consider this statement based on comments from individuals who possess Communication among their Signature Themes. It represents what Communication could "sound like."

"When I was a kid, I used to get in trouble for talking in class and clowning around. But when my classmates would laugh, it encouraged me to keep talking. My teachers said I was 'a joy to work with,' but that I was disrupting the class."

For further understanding of your talents, examine these five insights and select those that describe you best.

☐ You like to talk, and you are good at it.

☐ You can explain things and make them clear.

☐ You may have an ability to tell particularly captivating stories by constructing mental images in the minds of others.

☐ You may have been criticized because you like to talk a lot.

☐ Communication talents are valuable because your abilities in this area enable you to reach out and connect with people. Your story-telling ability builds images in the minds of others and makes you a powerful person as you connect and bond with people.

Competition as One of Your Signature Themes

To begin affirming Competition as one of your dominant areas of talent, first take another look at the description of that theme:

Competition is rooted in comparison. When you look at the world, you are instinctively aware of other people's performance. Their performance is the ultimate yardstick. No matter how hard you tried, no matter how worthy your intentions, if you reached your goal but did not outperform your peers, the achievement feels hollow. Like all competitors, you need other people. You need to compare. If you can compare, you can compete, and if you can compete, you can win. And when you win, there is no feeling quite like it. You like measurement because it facilitates comparisons. You like other competitors because they invigorate you. You like contests because they must produce a winner. You particularly like contests where you know you have the inside track to be the winner. Although you are gracious to your fellow competitors and even stoic in defeat, you don't compete for the fun of competing. You compete to win. Over time you will come to avoid contests where winning seems unlikely.

Now, consider this statement based on comments from individuals who possess Competition among their Signature Themes. It represents what Competition could "sound like."

"I truly am a competitive person. I always know 'the score,' and I always go for the win."

For further understanding of your talents, examine these five insights and select those that describe you best.

☐ You want to win, which usually means outperforming others.

☐ You will work very hard to excel past others.

☐ You constantly compare yourself and your performance to other people and their performances.

☐ You may not be willing to try something if you think you can't win. Other people may consider your competitiveness inappropriate and therefore push you away, reject you, or accuse you of being arrogant.

☐ Competition talents are valuable because through them you will influence and even push people in your group to achieve more than other groups. You bring energy to a group and can energize others to move to higher levels of excellence.

Connectedness as One of Your Signature Themes

To begin affirming Connectedness as one of your dominant areas of talent, first take another look at the description of that theme:

Things happen for a reason. You are sure of it. You are sure of it because in your soul you know that we are all connected. Yes, we are individuals, responsible for our own judgments and in possession of our own free will, but nonetheless we are part of something larger. Some may call it the collective unconscious. Others may label it spirit or life force. But whatever your word of choice, you gain confidence from knowing that we are not isolated from one another or from the earth and the life on it. This feeling of Connectedness implies certain responsibilities. If we are all part of a larger picture, then we must not harm others because we will be harming ourselves. We must not exploit because we will be exploiting ourselves. Your awareness of these responsibilities creates your value system. You are considerate, caring, and accepting. Certain of the unity of humankind, you are a bridge builder for people of different cultures. Sensitive to the invisible hand, you can give others comfort that there is a purpose beyond our humdrum lives. The exact articles of your faith will depend on your upbringing and your culture, but your faith is strong. It sustains you and your close friends in the face of life's mysteries.

Now, consider this statement based on comments from individuals who possess Connectedness among their Signature Themes. It represents what Connectedness could "sound like."

"I recently received an 1898 Indian Head penny in change, and immediately began wondering about the many times it had changed hands through the years. What path had this penny taken to reach me? Had a young child once carried it as a shiny new penny in his pocket, anxious to spend it at the candy store?"

For further understanding of your talents, examine these five insights and select those that describe you best.

☐ You see that all things happen for a reason. All things are working together in a purposeful manner.

☐ You feel connected to life itself. Therefore, you feel a responsibility to be considerate, caring, and accepting toward others.

☐ You are a bridge builder for people from all backgrounds to come together and develop a faith that goes beyond themselves.

☐ When people and the world seem fractured, broken, and isolated, you become discouraged and sometimes distressed. For this reason, some may perceive you as too naïve or fragile.

☐ Connectedness talents are valuable because they provide you with conviction and faith that sustain and encourage you and your friends in difficult times. You believe that there's a plan, a design, and a power beyond the visible world that provide meaning, comfort, and confidence. Your Connectedness gives you hope and helps you to achieve your ultimate goals.

Consistency as One of Your Signature Themes

To begin affirming Consistency as one of your dominant areas of talent, first take another look at the description of that theme:

Balance is important to you. You are keenly aware of the need to treat people the same, no matter what their station in life, so you do not want to see the scales tipped too far in any one person's favor. In your view this leads to selfishness and individualism. It leads to a world where some people gain an unfair advantage because of their connections or their background or their greasing of the wheels. This is truly offensive to you. You see yourself as a guardian against it. In direct contrast to this world of special favors, you believe that people function best in a consistent environment where the rules are clear and are applied to everyone equally. This is an environment where people know what is expected. It is predictable and evenhanded. It is fair. Here each person has an even chance to show his or her worth.

Now, consider this statement based on comments from individuals who possess Consistency among their Signature Themes. It represents what Consistency could "sound like."

"In one of my classes, we were each assigned a different book to read. But some of the books had 300 pages, while others had only 100. I wasn't very happy about that because I thought everyone should have to read the same book, or at least the same number of pages."

For further understanding of your talents, examine these five insights and select those that describe you best.

☐ You try to treat everyone consistently by having clear rules and treating everyone the same.

☐ You are offended when some people gain an advantage because of their connections or the games they play.

☐ You believe that people work best in a consistent environment where the rules apply to everyone equally, and you work to create that type of environment.

☐ While you may see yourself as a guardian of what is right and a warrior against special treatment, some people may reject you for assuming that responsibility.

☐ Consistency talents are valuable because you can more easily recognize inconsistencies, and you can readily suggest changes that can create a more equitable world.

Context as One of Your Signature Themes

To begin affirming Context as one of your dominant areas of talent, first take another look at the description of that theme:

You look back. You look back because that is where the answers lie. You look back to understand the present. From your vantage point the present is unstable, a confusing clamor of competing voices. It is only by casting your mind back to an earlier time, a time when the plans were being drawn up, that the present regains its stability. The earlier time was a simpler time. It was a time of blueprints. As you look back, you begin to see these blueprints emerge. You realize what the initial intentions were. These blueprints or intentions have since become so embellished that they are almost unrecognizable, but now this Context theme reveals them again. This understanding brings you confidence. No longer disoriented, you make better decisions because you sense the underlying structure. You become a better partner because you understand how your colleagues came to be who they are. And counterintuitively you become wiser about the future because you saw its seeds being sown in the past. Faced with new people and new situations, it will take you a little time to orient yourself, but you must give yourself this time. You must discipline yourself to ask the questions and allow the blueprints to emerge because no matter what the situation, if you haven't seen the blueprints, you will have less confidence in your decisions.

Now, consider this statement based on comments from individuals who possess Context among their Signature Themes. It represents what Context could "sound like."

"I need to read about how countries and their governments came into existence. I can't just watch today's world news and expect to fully understand it without knowing the history behind it."

For further understanding of your talents, examine these five insights and select those that describe you best.

☐ You look to the past to understand the present.

☐ You see patterns that emerge from studying what happened before.

☐ You learn best when you place what is to be learned into the context of other important dynamics and the history of what you are learning.

☐ You may feel disoriented when you can't see patterns stemming from the past. Others may become impatient with you as you strive to build an understanding of life's many complexities. You may be perceived as "slow" because you want to understand how we got to where we are.

☐ Context talents are valuable because they provide perspective that enhances your ability and confidence in making decisions and action planning.

Deliberative as One of Your Signature Themes

To begin affirming Deliberative as one of your dominant areas of talent, first take another look at the description of that theme:

You are careful. You are vigilant. You are a private person. You know that the world is an unpredictable place. Everything may seem in order, but beneath the surface you sense the many risks. Rather than denying these risks, you draw each one out into the open. Then each risk can be identified, assessed, and ultimately reduced. Thus, you are a fairly serious person who approaches life with a certain reserve. For example, you like to plan ahead so as to anticipate what might go wrong. You select your friends cautiously and keep your own counsel when the conversation turns to personal matters. You are careful not to give too much praise and recognition, lest it be misconstrued. If some people don't like you because you are not as effusive as others, then so be it. For you, life is not a popularity contest. Life is something of a minefield. Others can run through it recklessly if they so choose, but you take a different approach. You identify the dangers, weigh their relative impact, and then place your feet deliberately. You walk with care.

Now, consider this statement based on comments from individuals who possess Deliberative among their Signature Themes. It represents what Deliberative could "sound like."

"That seems like a good suggestion for my term paper, but I'd probably better think about it on my own for a while. I want make sure that enough resource materials are available — and I really ought to consider any other options before making a decision. There may be something I'm overlooking."

For further understanding of your talents, examine these five insights and select those that describe you best.

☐ You take great care as you consider options, thinking through the pros and cons of each alternative.

☐ To you, making the correct decision is more important than the time it takes to do so.

☐ You make very good decisions. In fact, you would change few of your choices or decisions.

☐ You may exhaust yourself and others as you make your decisions cautiously and slowly. You always think about the risks and what might go wrong. Therefore, some may falsely judge you as a pessimist. You may even be falsely categorized as less intelligent when in fact you are doing some very deep thinking.

☐ Deliberative talents are valuable because they enable you to eliminate or reduce errors by thoroughly considering each option. As a result, you make outstanding decisions.

Developer as One of Your Signature Themes

To begin affirming Developer as one of your dominant areas of talent, first take another look at the description of that theme:

You see the potential in others. Very often, in fact, potential is all you see. In your view no individual is fully formed. On the contrary, each individual is a work in progress, alive with possibilities. And you are drawn toward people for this very reason. When you interact with others, your goal is to help them experience success. You look for ways to challenge them. You devise interesting experiences that can stretch them and help them grow. And all the while you are on the lookout for the signs of growth — a new behavior learned or modified, a slight improvement in a skill, a glimpse of excellence or of "flow" where previously there were only halting steps. For you these small increments — invisible to some — are clear signs of potential being realized. These signs of growth in others are your fuel. They bring you strength and satisfaction. Over time many will seek you out for help and encouragement because on some level they know that your helpfulness is both genuine and fulfilling to you.

Now, consider this statement based on comments from individuals who possess Developer among their Signature Themes. It represents what Developer could "sound like."

"I am so excited about becoming a teacher. I look at children and see how much of a future they have, and I just love those moments when I see a child make even just a little bit of progress. That's my reward."

For further understanding of your talents, examine these five insights and select those that describe you best.

- ☐ You can see how other people can move, change, grow, and develop for the better.
- ☐ You love to see others make progress, and you will notice even the slightest progress.
- ☐ When you are a part of someone's development, it is the best experience in the world for you.
- ☐ Other people may not be as interested or ready to make the progress that you want them to make. Therefore, you may become frustrated when people don't want to improve, and you may feel frustrated or hurt when other people push you away because they feel pressured to improve.
- ☐ Developer talents are valuable because they help you see the potential in others and move them in that direction. People usually grow and improve in the presence of a developer. When you fully apply

your Developer talents, it is as if you are educating, counseling, and encouraging people all the time.

Discipline as One of Your Signature Themes

To begin affirming Discipline as one of your dominant areas of talent, first take another look at the description of that theme:

Your world needs to be predictable. It needs to be ordered and planned. So you instinctively impose structure on your world. You set up routines. You focus on timelines and deadlines. You break long-term projects into a series of specific short-term plans, and you work through each plan diligently. You are not necessarily neat and clean, but you do need precision. Faced with the inherent messiness of life, you want to feel in control. The routines, the timelines, the structure, all of these help create this feeling of control. Lacking this theme of Discipline, others may sometimes resent your need for order, but there need not be conflict. You must understand that not everyone feels your urge for predictability; they have other ways of getting things done. Likewise, you can help them understand and even appreciate your need for structure. Your dislike of surprises, your impatience with errors, your routines, and your detail orientation don't need to be misinterpreted as controlling behaviors that box people in. Rather, these behaviors can be understood as your instinctive method for maintaining your progress and your productivity in the face of life's many distractions.

Now, consider this statement based on comments from individuals who possess Discipline among their Signature Themes. It represents what Discipline could "sound like."

"Why do alarm clocks even have snooze buttons? Set your alarm for the time you want to get up. Then, when your alarm goes off, get up!"

For further understanding of your talents, examine these five insights and select those that describe you best.

☐ You find ways to organize yourself to get things done on time.

☐ You tend to place yourself in productive environments.

☐ You create order and structure where it is needed.

☐ Some people may label you as compulsive, anal, or a control freak because of your ability to discipline yourself and structure your world. But these attributes make you productive — usually more so than your critics.

☐ Discipline talents are valuable because they make you efficient *and* effective. First, they first motivate you to organize tasks. Then, they keep you motivated to complete those tasks.

Empathy as One of Your Signature Themes

To begin affirming Empathy as one of your dominant areas of talent, first take another look at the description of that theme:

You can sense the emotions of those around you. You can feel what they are feeling as though their feelings are your own. Intuitively, you are able to see the world through their eyes and share their perspective. You do not necessarily agree with each person's perspective. You do not necessarily feel pity for each person's predicament — this would be sympathy, not Empathy. You do not necessarily condone the choices each person makes, but you do understand. This instinctive ability to understand is powerful. You hear the unvoiced questions. You anticipate the need. Where others grapple for words, you seem to find the right words and the right tone. You help people find the right phrases to express their feelings — to themselves as well as to others. You help them give voice to their emotional life. For all these reasons other people are drawn to you.

Now, consider this statement based on comments from individuals who possess Empathy among their Signature Themes. It represents what Empathy could "sound like."

"A friend of mine recently adopted a child. I was very happy for her, but the night before the adoption, all I could think of was the birth mother's pain in having to give up her five-month-old child.

I just knew she was clutching her child and shedding tears, and I cried with her."

For further understanding of your talents, examine these five insights and select those that describe you best.

☐ You can sense what it feels like to be someone else.

☐ You can pick up on the pain and joy of others — sometimes before they express it. Other people feel heard by you and experience your compassion.

☐ Because you can quickly understand others, people are drawn to you when they have a need or a problem, especially in relationships.

☐ Your Empathy can be challenging because you may become overwhelmed with all of the emotions you can pick up in a day. Roles and relationships in which people project their negative emotions your way are hard on you. You can become exhausted from the emotions you pick up from others.

☐ Empathy talents are valuable because they enable you to form very close, supportive relationships in which you help and encourage others.

Focus as One of Your Signature Themes

To begin affirming Focus as one of your dominant areas of talent, first take another look at the description of that theme:

"Where am I headed?" you ask yourself. You ask this question every day. Guided by this theme of Focus, you need a clear destination. Lacking one, your life and your work can quickly become frustrating. And so each year, each month, and even each week you set goals. These goals then serve as your compass, helping you determine priorities and make the necessary corrections to get back on course. Your Focus is powerful because it forces you to filter; you instinctively evaluate whether or not a particular action will help you move toward your goal. Those that don't are ignored. In the end, then, your Focus forces you to be efficient. Naturally, the flip side of this is that it causes you to become impatient with delays, obstacles, and even tangents, no matter how intriguing they appear to be. This makes you an extremely valuable team member. When others start to wander down other avenues, you bring them back to the main road. Your Focus reminds everyone that if something is not helping you move toward your destination, then it is not important. And if it is not important, then it is not worth your time. You keep everyone on point.

Now, consider this statement based on comments from individuals who possess Focus among their Signature Themes. It represents what Focus could "sound like."

"Sometimes I'm so intent on my homework that my roommate can walk into the room, stand right beside me, and say my name — and I don't even realize he's there. I get so zoned in on what I'm doing that nothing breaks my concentration."

For further understanding of your talents, examine these five insights and select those that describe you best.

☐ You can take a direction, follow through, and make the necessary corrections to stay on track.

☐ You prioritize your life and tasks, and then you take action.

☐ You set goals that keep you effective and efficient.

☐ You become frustrated when you can't determine what a group is trying to do. Likewise, your life and work become frustrating when your goals are unclear.

☐ Focus talents are valuable because you can quickly evaluate, determine priorities, and get yourself and groups on track quickly. Your Focus motivates you to be efficient. You get a lot done because you don't get easily distracted.

Futuristic as One of Your Signature Themes

To begin affirming Futuristic as one of your dominant areas of talent, first take another look at the description of that theme:

"Wouldn't it be great if . . ." You are the kind of person who loves to peer over the horizon. The future fascinates you. As if it were projected on the wall, you see in detail what the future might hold, and this detailed picture keeps pulling you forward, into tomorrow. While the exact content of the picture will depend on your other strengths and interests — a better product, a better team, a better life, or a better world — it will always be inspirational to you. You are a dreamer who sees visions of what could be and who cherishes those visions. When the present proves too frustrating and the people around you too pragmatic, you conjure up your visions of the future and they energize you. They can energize others, too. In fact, very often people look to you to describe your visions of the future. They want a picture that can raise their sights and thereby their spirits. You can paint it for them. Practice. Choose your words carefully. Make the picture as vivid as possible. People will want to latch on to the hope you bring.

Now, consider this statement based on comments from individuals who possess Futuristic among their Signature Themes. It represents what Futuristic could "sound like."

"I'm majoring in engineering because I intend to become a city planner. I know that five years from now our city will be experiencing tremendous growth, and I already have ideas about how to accommodate that growth while improving the quality of life."

For further understanding of your talents, examine these five insights and select those that describe you best.

☐ You are fascinated by the future, and you usually see the future positively.

☐ You can see in detail what the future might hold.

☐ You can energize yourself and others by your vision of what could be. You can clearly see possibilities.

☐ Others may dismiss you as a dreamer. You may become frustrated by present circumstances and discouraged by highly pragmatic people who can't or won't see the possibilities in the future that are so clear to you.

☐ Futuristic talents are valuable because your vision raises others' sights and focuses their energies.

Harmony as One of Your Signature Themes

To begin affirming Harmony as one of your dominant areas of talent, first take another look at the description of that theme:

You look for areas of agreement. In your view there is little to be gained from conflict and friction, so you seek to hold them to a minimum. When you know that the people around you hold differing views, you try to find the common ground. You try to steer them away from confrontation and toward harmony. In fact, harmony is one of your guiding values. You can't quite believe how much time is wasted by people trying to impose their views on others. Wouldn't we all be more productive if we kept our opinions in check and instead looked for consensus and support? You believe we would, and you live by that belief. When others are sounding off about their goals, their claims, and their fervently held opinions, you hold your peace. When others strike out in a direction, you will willingly, in the service of harmony, modify your own objectives to merge with theirs (as long as their basic values do not clash with yours). When others start to argue about their pet theory or concept, you steer clear of the debate, preferring to talk about practical, down-to-earth matters on which you can all agree. In your view we are all in the same boat, and we need this boat to get where we are going. It is a good boat. There is no need to rock it just to show that you can.

Now, consider this statement based on comments from individuals who possess Harmony among their Signature Themes. It represents what Harmony could "sound like."

"I know that I should have said something to the waiter about my steak not being cooked correctly, but I really didn't want to raise a fuss and ruin the evening."

For further understanding of your talents, examine these five insights and select those that describe you best.

☐ You want peace, and you try to bring people together.

☐ You can see points that people have in common, even when they are in conflict.

☐ You seek to help individuals, families, and organizations work together.

☐ Some people may criticize you or misunderstand you. They may say that you lack courage. You too may see your desire for harmony as only an avoidance of conflict.

☐ Harmony talents are valuable because you see what people have in common and try to help them to interact on the basis of shared points of view. This binds people to you and helps groups come together. Groups, organizations, and teams function better and achieve more because of what you do to bring people together.

Ideation as One of Your Signature Themes

To begin affirming Ideation as one of your dominant areas of talent, first take another look at the description of that theme:

You are fascinated by ideas. What is an idea? An idea is a concept, the best explanation of the most events. You are delighted when you discover beneath the complex surface an elegantly simple concept to explain why things are the way they are. An idea is a connection. Yours is the kind of mind that is always looking for connections, and so you are intrigued when seemingly disparate phenomena can be linked by an obscure connection. An idea is a new perspective on familiar challenges. You revel in taking the world we all know and turning it around so we can view it from a strange but strangely enlightening angle. You love all these ideas because they are profound, because they are novel, because they are clarifying, because they are contrary, because they are bizarre. For all these reasons you derive a jolt of energy whenever a new idea occurs to you. Others may label you creative or original or conceptual or even smart. Perhaps you are all of these. Who can be sure? What you are sure of is that ideas are thrilling. And on most days this is enough.

Now, consider this statement based on comments from individuals who possess Ideation among their Signature Themes. It represents what Ideation could "sound like."

"I proposed my own assignment to my professor in lieu of the one she gave us. Instead of writing a research paper on the Irish potato famine, I asked permission to write a one-act play about it."

For further understanding of your talents, examine these five insights and select those that describe you best.

☐ You are a creative person, and you appreciate originality.

☐ You like free-thinking experiences such as brainstorming and discussion groups.

☐ You love new ideas and concepts.

☐ At times, it may seem like you get lost in the world of ideas, and others may think you are a little "spacey."

☐ Ideation talents are valuable because they enable you to look for new connections and generate new insights when things don't make sense. You are able to help others take the world they know and turn it around so that they can see it from a new point of view.

Includer as One of Your Signature Themes

To begin affirming Includer as one of your dominant areas of talent, first take another look at the description of that theme:

"Stretch the circle wider." This is the philosophy around which you orient your life. You want to include people and make them feel part of the group. In direct contrast to those who are drawn only to exclusive groups, you actively avoid those groups that exclude others. You want to expand the group so that as many people as possible can benefit from its support. You hate the sight of someone on the outside looking in. You want to draw them in so that they can feel the warmth of the group. You are an instinctively accepting person. Regardless of race or sex or nationality or personality or faith, you cast few judgments. Judgments can hurt a person's feelings. Why do that if you don't have to? Your accepting nature does not necessarily rest on a belief that each of us is different and that one should respect these differences. Rather, it rests on your conviction that fundamentally we are all the same. We are all equally important. Thus, no one should be ignored. Each of us should be included. It is the least we all deserve.

Now, consider this statement based on comments from individuals who possess Includer among their Signature Themes. It represents what Includer could "sound like."

"Staci suggested that we form a study group to prepare for the final exam, and I think it's a great idea. Why don't we get the whole class together?"

For further understanding of your talents, examine these five insights and select those that describe you best.

☐ You notice people who feel like outsiders or who feel unappreciated.

☐ You are not content when people are left out, so you try to reach out to the "outsiders," and you try to bring them in.

☐ People see you as accepting and sense that you want them to be included.

☐ In your attempts to include others, you may be rejected by the very people you try to include. You may have to confront your own fears as you seek to include those who may reject you. You may also have to deal with people who misunderstand your actions and yet do nothing to reach out to those who feel left out.

☐ Includer talents are valuable because they enable you to help individuals, groups, organizations, and communities to be unified and effective. People who have felt rejected will appreciate your efforts.

Individualization as One of Your Signature Themes

To begin affirming Individualization as one of your dominant areas of talent, first take another look at the description of that theme:

Your Individualization theme leads you to be intrigued by the unique qualities of each person. You are impatient with generalizations or "types" because you don't want to obscure what is special and distinct about each person. Instead, you focus on the differences between individuals. You instinctively observe each person's style, each person's motivation, how each thinks, and how each builds relationships. You hear the one-of-a-kind stories in each person's life. This theme explains why you pick your friends just the right birthday gift, why you know that one person prefers praise in public and another detests it, and why you tailor your teaching style to accommodate one person's need to be shown and another's desire to "figure it out as I go." Because you are such a keen observer of other people's strengths, you can draw out the best in each person. This Individualization theme also helps you build productive teams. While some search around for the perfect team "structure" or "process," you know instinctively that the secret to great teams is casting by individual strengths so that everyone can do a lot of what they do well.

Now, consider this statement based on comments from individuals who possess Individualization among their Signature Themes. It represents what Individualization could "sound like."

"I volunteered to chair the Earth Day committee, partially because I want to be sure that we have the right people in the right roles. Joe is an accounting major, so I knew he'd be helpful in handling the budget, and Kelly would be good at promoting the event because she knows so many people on campus."

For further understanding of your talents, examine these five insights and select those that describe you best.

☐ You see each person as a distinct, one-of-a-kind individual.

☐ You can see how people who are very different can work together.

☐ You can build productive teams of people because you can see the talents of people and then structure groups around those talents.

☐ Because you see individuals so distinctly and try to relate to them in terms of their specific characteristics, relating to people can be taxing and even overwhelming.

☐ Individualization talents are valuable because they help you form powerful relationships with people. Those people know that you take them seriously and that you see them as distinct individuals. For many, this is very valuable, as it brings trust and intensity to your relationships.

Input as One of Your Signature Themes

To begin affirming Input as one of your dominant areas of talent, first take another look at the description of that theme:

You are inquisitive. You collect things. You might collect information — words, facts, books, and quotations — or you might collect tangible objects such as butterflies, baseball cards, porcelain dolls, or sepia photographs. Whatever you collect, you collect it because it interests you. And yours is the kind of mind that finds so many things interesting. The world is exciting precisely because of its infinite variety and complexity. If you read a great deal, it is not necessarily to refine your theories but, rather, to add more information to your archives. If you like to travel, it is because each new location offers novel artifacts and facts. These can be acquired and then stored away. Why are they worth storing? At the time of storing it is often hard to say exactly when or why you might need them, but who knows when they might become useful? With all those possible uses in mind, you really don't feel comfortable throwing anything away. So you keep acquiring and compiling and filing stuff away. It's interesting. It keeps your mind fresh. And perhaps one day some of it will prove valuable.

Now, consider this statement based on comments from individuals who possess Input among their Signature Themes. It represents what Input could "sound like."

"Whenever I read magazines, I always tear out pictures of home designs that I like. I'm not really ready to buy a house, but someday I might, and these ideas might come in handy."

For further understanding of your talents, examine these five insights and select those that describe you best.

☐ You always want to know more. You crave information.

☐ You like to collect certain things, such as ideas, books, memorabilia, quotations, and facts.

☐ You have an active curiosity. You find many things very interesting.

☐ You may have difficulty getting started or completing a project because you feel like you never have enough information. Going to a library or "surfing the Net" may turn into hours once your curiosity takes off, and you may have difficulties filing and housing all of the new information and ideas you acquire.

☐ Input talents are valuable because they keep your mind active and lead you to become knowledgeable. You are likely to become an expert in one or more areas.

Intellection as One of Your Signature Themes

To begin affirming Intellection as one of your dominant areas of talent, first take another look at the description of that theme:

You like to think. You like mental activity. You like exercising the "muscles" of your brain, stretching them in multiple directions. This need for mental activity may be focused; for example, you may be trying to solve a problem or develop an idea or understand another person's feelings. The exact focus will depend on your other strengths. On the other hand, this mental activity may very well lack focus. The theme of Intellection does not dictate what you are thinking about; it simply describes that you like to think. You are the kind of person who enjoys your time alone because it is your time for musing and reflection. You are introspective. In a sense you are your own best companion, as you pose yourself questions and try out answers on yourself to see how they sound. This introspection may lead you to a slight sense of discontent as you compare what you are actually doing with all the thoughts and ideas that your mind conceives. Or this introspection may tend toward more pragmatic matters such as the events of the day or a conversation that you plan to have later. Wherever it leads you, this mental hum is one of the constants of your life.

Now, consider this statement based on comments from individuals who possess Intellection among their Signature Themes. It represents what Intellection could "sound like."

"I once got to house-sit for one of my professors. The time away from all the noise and activity at the dorm was a great opportunity to think about the best way to approach the rest of the semester."

For further understanding of your talents, examine these five insights and select those that describe you best.

☐ You love to study, and you prefer intellectual discussions.

☐ You like to think and to let your thoughts go in many directions.

☐ You like to spend time alone so that you can reflect and ponder.

☐ You may become discouraged because there are so many things that you need to think about so carefully and thoroughly.

☐ Intellection talents are valuable because they help you find innovative ideas and solutions.

Learner as One of Your Signature Themes

To begin affirming Learner as one of your dominant areas of talent, first take another look at the description of that theme:

You love to learn. The subject matter that interests you most will be determined by your other themes and experiences, but whatever the subject, you will always be drawn to the process of learning. The process, more than the content or the result, is especially exciting for you. You are energized by the steady and deliberate journey from ignorance to competence. The thrill of the first few facts, the early efforts to recite or practice what you have learned, the growing confidence of a skill mastered — this is the process that entices you. Your excitement leads you to engage in adult learning experiences — yoga or piano lessons or graduate classes. It enables you to thrive in dynamic work environments where you are asked to take on short project assignments and are expected to learn a lot about the new subject matter in a short period of time and then move on to the next one. This Learner theme does not necessarily mean that you seek to become the subject matter expert, or that you are striving for the respect that accompanies a professional or academic credential. The outcome of the learning is less significant than the "getting there."

Now, consider this statement based on comments from individuals who possess Learner among their Signature Themes. It represents what Learner could "sound like."

"I'm studying Italian, even though I don't know anyone who speaks it, and I'll probably never have much of an opportunity to use it. It's just a great way for me to feel mentally stimulated and to keep growing as a person — and it satisfies my curiosity."

For further understanding of your talents, examine these five insights and select those that describe you best.

☐ You want to continuously learn and improve.

☐ You enjoy the process of learning as much as what you actually learn.

☐ You get a thrill out of learning new facts, beginning a new subject, and mastering an important skill. Learning builds your confidence.

☐ You can get frustrated about wanting to learn so many different things because you fear you'll never be an expert.

☐ Learner talents are valuable because they propel you to thrive in a dynamic world where learning is a necessity. You can learn a lot in a short period of time.

Maximizer as One of Your Signature Themes

To begin affirming Maximizer as one of your dominant areas of talent, first take another look at the description of that theme:

Excellence, not average, is your measure. Taking something from below average to slightly above average takes a great deal of effort and in your opinion is not very rewarding. Transforming something strong into something superb takes just as much effort but is much more thrilling. Strengths, whether yours or someone else's, fascinate you. Like a diver after pearls, you search them out, watching for the telltale signs of a strength. A glimpse of untutored excellence, rapid learning, a skill mastered without recourse to steps — all these are clues that a strength may be in play. And having found a strength, you feel compelled to nurture it, refine it, and stretch it toward excellence. You polish the pearl until it shines. This natural sorting of strengths means that others see you as discriminating. You choose to spend time with people who appreciate your particular strengths. Likewise, you are attracted to others who seem to have found and cultivated their own strengths. You tend to avoid those who want to fix you and make you well rounded. You don't want to spend your life bemoaning what you lack. Rather, you want to capitalize on the gifts with which you are blessed. It's more fun. It's more productive. And, counterintuitively, it is more demanding.

Now, consider this statement based on comments from individuals who possess Maximizer among their Signature Themes. It represents what Maximizer could "sound like."

"Our design for the engineering project has been getting great reviews, but let's consider programming some special features into it. We have the time, so there's no reason why we shouldn't make it even better."

For further understanding of your talents, examine these five insights and select those that describe you best.

☐ You see talents and strengths in others, sometimes before they do.

☐ You love to help others become excited by the potential of their natural talents.

☐ You have the capacity to see what people will do best and which jobs they will be good at. You can see how people's talents match the tasks that must be completed.

☐ Some people will be intimidated by your perceptiveness and drive for excellence. These people may want to keep you at a distance, and you may feel rejected or like there is something wrong with you.

☐ Maximizer talents are valuable because they help you focus on talents to stimulate personal and group excellence. If a group or organization is on the move toward excellence, a talented Maximizer is probably somewhere in the midst.

Positivity as One of Your Signature Themes

To begin affirming Positivity as one of your dominant areas of talent, first take another look at the description of that theme:

You are generous with praise, quick to smile, and always on the lookout for the positive in the situation. Some call you lighthearted. Others just wish that their glass were as full as yours seems to be. But either way, people want to be around you. Their world looks better around you because your enthusiasm is contagious. Lacking your energy and optimism, some find their world drab with repetition or, worse, heavy with pressure. You seem to find a way to lighten their spirit. You inject drama into every project. You celebrate every achievement. You find ways to make everything more exciting and more vital. Some cynics may reject your energy, but you are rarely dragged down. Your Positivity won't allow it. Somehow you can't quite escape your conviction that it is good to be alive, that work can be fun, and that no matter what the setbacks, one must never lose one's sense of humor.

Now, consider this statement based on comments from individuals who possess Positivity among their Signature Themes. It represents what Positivity could "sound like."

"The road construction that's being done on my daily route to work has given me a great opportunity. I get to take to take a different route through some small towns and rolling farmland. It's beautiful."

For further understanding of your talents, examine these five insights and select those that describe you best.

☐ You bring enthusiasm to people, groups, and organizations.

☐ You can stimulate people to be more productive and become more hopeful.

☐ You can get people excited about what they are doing, and therefore they become more productive.

☐ Some people will criticize you for being so optimistic. They may say you are naïve, and that may cause you to doubt yourself.

☐ Positivity talents are valuable because they have such a helpful influence on the attitudes, motivation, and productive behaviors of others. Groups and individuals are energized to move toward excellence.

Relator as One of Your Signature Themes

To begin affirming Relator as one of your dominant areas of talent, first take another look at the description of that theme:

Relator describes your attitude toward your relationships. In simple terms, the Relator theme pulls you toward people you already know. You do not necessarily shy away from meeting new people — in fact, you may have other themes that cause you to enjoy the thrill of turning strangers into friends — but you do derive a great deal of pleasure and strength from being around your close friends. You are comfortable with intimacy. Once the initial connection has been made, you deliberately encourage a deepening of the relationship. You want to understand their feelings, their goals, their fears, and their dreams; and you want them to understand yours. You know that this kind of closeness implies a certain amount of risk — you might be taken advantage of — but you are willing to accept that risk. For you a relationship has value only if it is genuine. And the only way to know that is to entrust yourself to the other person. The more you share with each other, the more you risk together. The more you risk together, the more each of you proves your caring is genuine. These are your steps toward real friendship, and you take them willingly.

Now, consider this statement based on comments from individuals who possess Relator among their Signature Themes. It represents what Relator could "sound like."

"Leaving all my high school friends behind when I started college was hard. Even though I'm meeting a bunch of people here, they're still only acquaintances. There's such a big difference between being friendly with people and actually being friends."

For further understanding of your talents, examine these five insights and select those that describe you best.

☐ You can form close relationships with people, and you enjoy doing so.

☐ You receive profound satisfaction from working hard with friends to accomplish an important goal.

☐ You know many people, and you can relate with all kinds of people. But you also have a very small group of friends with whom you have an incredibly deep relationship.

☐ Some people may feel threatened or uncomfortable because they can't bring themselves to have the close, intense personal relationships that you thrive on.

☐ Relator talents are valuable to organizations, groups, and individuals because they foster interpersonal relationships that lead to productivity.

Responsibility as One of Your Signature Themes

To begin affirming Responsibility as one of your dominant areas of talent, first take another look at the description of that theme:

Your Responsibility theme forces you to take psychological ownership for anything you commit to, and whether large or small, you feel emotionally bound to follow it through to completion. Your good name depends on it. If for some reason you cannot deliver, you automatically start to look for ways to make it up to the other person. Apologies are not enough. Excuses and rationalizations are totally unacceptable. You will not quite be able to live with yourself until you have made restitution. This conscientiousness, this near obsession for doing things right, and your impeccable ethics, combine to create your reputation: utterly dependable. When assigning new responsibilities, people will look to you first because they know it will get done. When people come to you for help — and they soon will — you must be selective. Your willingness to volunteer may sometimes lead you to take on more than you should.

Now, consider this statement based on comments from individuals who possess Responsibility among their Signature Themes. It represents what Responsibility could "sound like."

"I'm picky about who I work with. I need to know that they are going to follow through on their commitments and do what they say they will do. People rely on me to be responsible, so I expect my teammates to be responsible, too."

For further understanding of your talents, examine these five insights and select those that describe you best.

☐ You are dependable, and people know that they can count on you.

☐ You don't want to let people down, and you will work very hard to fulfill all your responsibilities and keep your word.

☐ You have many obligations and commitments because so many people know that they can count on you. Therefore, more and more people come to you.

☐ With the responsibility you feel to the people who come to you and with the demands that each of them brings, you often feel overwhelmed and under pressure to perform.

☐ Responsibility talents are valuable because they lead others to trust you and to become more responsible themselves. You might be more of a role model than you realize.

Restorative as One of Your Signature Themes

To begin affirming Restorative as one of your dominant areas of talent, first take another look at the description of that theme:

You love to solve problems. Whereas some are dismayed when they encounter yet another breakdown, you can be energized by it. You enjoy the challenge of analyzing the symptoms, identifying what is wrong, and finding the solution. You may prefer practical problems or conceptual ones or personal ones. You may seek out specific kinds of problems that you have met many times before and that you are confident you can fix. Or you may feel the greatest push when faced with complex and unfamiliar problems. Your exact preferences are determined by your other themes and experiences. But what is certain is that you enjoy bringing things back to life. It is a wonderful feeling to identify the undermining factor(s), eradicate them, and restore something to its true glory. Intuitively, you know that without your intervention, this thing — this machine, this technique, this person, this company — might have ceased to function. You fixed it, resuscitated it, rekindled its vitality. Phrasing it the way you might, you saved it.

Now, consider this statement based on comments from individuals who possess Restorative among their Signature Themes. It represents what

Restorative could "sound like."

"My favorite computers are those that aren't working. I love finding computers that people have thrown out and rebuilding them. But once one is rebuilt, I just give it away or sell it. I'd rather salvage another broken one than keep tinkering with one that already works."

For further understanding of your talents, examine these five insights and select those that describe you best.

☐ You readily take on projects that others believe "can't be saved."

☐ You can analyze a situation and identify potential shortcomings and what needs to be fixed.

☐ You quickly recognize problems that others may not detect.

☐ Other people may not like the fact that you can so quickly determine the problems and weaknesses in people, situations, and organizations. They may find this ability embarrassing, even if your assessments and solutions are accurate.

☐ Restorative talents are valuable because through them you are energized, rather than defeated, by problems.

Self-Assurance as One of Your Signature Themes

To begin affirming Self-Assurance as one of your dominant areas of talent, first take another look at the description of that theme:

Self-Assurance is similar to self-confidence. In the deepest part of you, you have faith in your strengths. You know that you are able — able to take risks, able to meet new challenges, able to stake claims, and, most important, able to deliver. But Self-Assurance is more than just self-confidence. Blessed with the theme of Self-Assurance, you have confidence not only in your abilities but in your judgment. When you look at the world, you know that your perspective is unique and distinct. And because no one sees exactly what you see, you know that no one can make your decisions for you. No one can tell you what to think. They can guide. They can suggest. But you alone have the authority to form conclusions, make decisions, and act. This authority, this final accountability for the living of your life, does not intimidate you. On the contrary, it feels natural to you. No matter what the situation, you seem to know what the right decision is. This theme lends you an aura of certainty. Unlike many, you are not easily swayed by someone else's arguments, no matter how persuasive they may be. This Self-Assurance may be quiet or loud, depending on your other themes, but it is solid. It is strong. Like the keel of a ship, it withstands many different pressures and keeps you on your course.

Now, consider this statement based on comments from individuals who possess Self-Assurance among their Signature Themes. It represents what Self-Assurance could "sound like."

"I tried out for the baseball team last year and didn't make it. But I'm going to try again this year — and in my gut I know I'm going to make it. I believe in myself. The same thing happened in high school. I've done it once; I know I can do it again."

For further understanding of your talents, examine these five insights and select those that describe you best.

☐ You are confident about your ability to manage your life.

☐ You can "bounce back" from disappointments and crises.

☐ You believe that your decisions are right and that your perspective is unique and distinct.

☐ Other people may see your self-assurance as a type of pride or arrogance. Some people may criticize you when they wish that they had your confidence. Sometimes people want to get close to you because they hope that some of your confidence will rub off on them. But other people will keep you away because they don't have your confidence and are afraid that you will see through them.

☐ Self-Assurance talents are valuable because they keep you strong as you withstand many pressures, as you stay on your course, and as you willingly claim the authority to form conclusions, make decisions, and act.

Significance as One of Your Signature Themes

To begin affirming Significance as one of your dominant areas of talent, first take another look at the description of that theme:

You want to be very significant in the eyes of other people. In the truest sense of the word you want to be recognized. You want to be heard. You want to stand out. You want to be known. In particular, you want to be known and appreciated for the unique strengths you bring. You feel a need to be admired as credible, professional, and successful. Likewise, you want to associate with others who are credible, professional, and successful. And if they aren't, you will push them to achieve until they are. Or you will move on. An independent spirit, you want your work to be a way of life rather than a job, and in that work you want to be given free rein, the leeway to do things your way. Your yearnings feel intense to you, and you honor those yearnings. And so your life is filled with goals, achievements, or qualifications that you crave. Whatever your focus — and each person is distinct — your Significance theme will keep pulling you upward, away from the mediocre toward the exceptional. It is the theme that keeps you reaching.

Now, consider this statement based on comments from individuals who possess Significance among their Signature Themes. It represents what Significance could "sound like."

"I want my professors to know my name. The last thing I want to do is fade into the crowd, and I can never receive too much recognition."

For further understanding of your talents, examine these five insights and select those that describe you best.

☐ You probably enjoy receiving public recognition for the differences you make.

☐ You want to have an impact on other people, groups, and society as a whole.

☐ You want the contributions you make to be viewed as substantial, powerful, and significant.

☐ Although many people will appreciate your talent in this theme, others may be intimidated by it, and they might not say so. Instead, they may say that you are "just wanting attention" or that you are "egocentric."

☐ Significance talents are valuable because they can be a source of energy for doing good and helpful things that will outlive you. You are motivated by a driving force to produce transformational, lasting change.

Strategic as One of Your Signature Themes

To begin affirming Strategic as one of your dominant areas of talent, first take another look at the description of that theme:

The Strategic theme enables you to sort through the clutter and find the best route. It is not a skill that can be taught. It is a distinct way of thinking, a special perspective on the world at large. This perspective allows you to see patterns where others simply see complexity. Mindful of these patterns, you play out alternative scenarios, always asking, "What if this happened? Okay, well what if this happened?" This recurring question helps you see around the next corner. There you can evaluate accurately the potential obstacles. Guided by where you see each path leading, you start to make selections. You discard the paths that lead nowhere. You discard the paths that lead straight into resistance. You discard the paths that lead into a fog of confusion. You cull and make selections until you arrive at the chosen path — your strategy. Armed with your strategy, you strike forward. This is your Strategic theme at work: "What if?" Select. Strike.

Now, consider this statement based on comments from individuals who possess Strategic among their Signature Themes. It represents what Strategic could "sound like."

"I chose this college to prepare for medical school. I'd like to do it as quickly as possible, so I considered trying to finish in three years.

But I want to get into a top school, so I'm going to limit the credit hours I take each semester and really get good grades."

For further understanding of your talents, examine these five insights and select those that describe you best.

☐ You create multiple ways to do things.

☐ You can quickly pick out the relevant issues and patterns when confronted by problems and complexities.

☐ You have a "What if this happens?" mentality toward work and life. This type of questioning helps you see, plan, and prepare for future situations.

☐ Some may criticize you for not moving on issues as quickly as they may like, but you know that there is great wisdom in reviewing all of the potential problems and searching for the alternative that will work best.

☐ Strategic talents are valuable because they enable you to quickly reach goals by seeing the pros and cons of various alternatives. You carefully consider the whole picture and then generate the most effective set of actions or routes to take.

Woo as One of Your Signature Themes

To begin affirming Woo as one of your dominant areas of talent, first take another look at the description of that theme:

Woo stands for winning others over. You enjoy the challenge of meeting new people and getting them to like you. Strangers are rarely intimidating to you. On the contrary, strangers can be energizing. You are drawn to them. You want to learn their names, ask them questions, and find some area of common interest so that you can strike up a conversation and build rapport. Some people shy away from starting up conversations because they worry about running out of things to say. You don't. Not only are you rarely at a loss for words; you actually enjoy initiating with strangers because you derive satisfaction from breaking the ice and making a connection. Once that connection is made, you are quite happy to wrap it up and move on. There are new people to meet, new rooms to work, new crowds to mingle in. In your world there are no strangers, only friends you haven't met yet — lots of them.

Now, consider this statement based on comments from individuals who possess Woo among their Signature Themes. It represents what Woo could "sound like."

"The first day of classes is always so fun. I made a lot of new friends today, and introduced myself to each of my professors!"

For further understanding of your talents, examine these five insights and select those that describe you best.

☐ You have the capacity to quickly connect with people and generate positive responses from them.

☐ You can enter a crowd of people and easily know what to do and what to say.

☐ You see no strangers, only friends you haven't met yet.

☐ Because you know so many people, some may believe that you form only shallow relationships. Others, however, will envy the way you make friends.

☐ Woo talents are valuable because people are influenced by your ability to draw them into a group or a relationship.

Chapter IV

SEEING THROUGH
STRENGTHS-COLORED GLASSES

B obby Televerde graduated from high school with a 2.54 grade-point average. He was ranked 189th in a class of 301 students. His SAT verbal was 390 (39th percentile), and his SAT math was 500 (57th percentile). His senior-year grades were the worst of his high school career: one A, but one C+, one C, two C-'s, one D+, three D's and two D-'s.

After high school, Bobby didn't know what to do with his life, so he went to a community college near his home. In his first year, he earned one A, two B's, and two F's, and he withdrew from three other classes. The next year, Bobby chose to attend a different community college in a neighboring city, but his performance and withdrawal pattern continued.

While attending these community colleges, Bobby worked as a manual laborer in a large warehouse. One day, as he entered the warehouse to begin working, he caught a view of the entire warehouse floor, capturing all of his fellow workers in one "snapshot."

Bobby was shocked by what he saw. He suddenly realized that he could be looking at his own future. Although he had been working at the warehouse for only two years, many of his coworkers had been there for 10, 20, or even 30 years. A career of manual labor at the warehouse was not Bobby's goal for himself.

He has never been the same since that defining moment. Bobby went back to his community college with a different perspective and a renewed determination. School wasn't easy. Bobby's academic skills were minimal, but with sheer will, he was determined to learn, change, and improve. He didn't know anything else but to work hard, so he did just that because he was determined to build a future outside of the warehouse.

Within a year, Bobby was earning all A's and B's. Two years later, his GPA was 3.4, and he was admitted to a major university. Three years later, Bobby graduated from that university with a grade-point average of 3.9. Bobby then focused on gaining admission to law school and scored in the 95th percentile on the law-school admissions test. He went on to one of the top law schools in the nation.

The Power of Perspective

The revolutionary change in Bobby Televerde's life is a testament to the power of having a vision of where you are and where you want to go. In the warehouse, Bobby saw how his life would likely unfold. That vision gave him a new perspective on life, and that new perspective changed everything.

Your own perspective on life can do the same thing for you. You've probably heard people criticized for looking at the world through "rose-colored glasses." Those making such judgments are saying, "You are being naïve. You are seeing things in an overly positive manner." But that is not the case. As Franklin Delano Roosevelt, 32nd President of the United States, said, "Men are not prisoners of fate, but only prisoners of their own minds."

We suggest that you should see the world through strengths-colored glasses — a revolutionary way of viewing yourself and those around you.

We live in a society and a time in history when people are preoccupied by who they *aren't*. People are obsessed with worries about not being smart enough, not being pretty enough, not being good enough, or not having a personality that's good enough.

The advertising industry has made a science out of focusing our attention on who we *aren't*. They know very well that if they can get us to believe that we are "not enough," they can set us up to buy virtually any product or service.

This book, along with the other components of the StrengthsQuest program, invites you to live from a strengths perspective. We want you to see yourself and others not in terms of what you may lack, but in terms of the tremendous value and potential held in your talent.

The Revolutionary Aspect of Seeing Through Strengths-Colored Glasses

From the moment you begin seeing life through strengths-colored glasses, things will change. And these changes will likely be revolutionary. Once you start seeing yourself in terms of your talents and strengths, a certain discontent may set in. Whereas in the past you may have been satisfied with a low level of performance, once you discover the potential held in your talents, you will likely begin to strive for excellence.

As you look at yourself from a strengths perspective, you will question how well you are using your talents.

Further, you will probably ask yourself how much you could accomplish if you developed your talents into strengths. Because developing a talent into a strength involves the addition of knowledge and skill, you will more than likely begin setting goals for your education — goals that will help you fulfill the potential of your talents.

But the revolution won't stop with you. Your strengths-colored glasses will likely give you a different perspective on other people and revolutionize your relationships. You'll find yourself asking questions to determine the talents and strengths of those you love, and you will want them to see themselves from a strengths perspective, too. You'll find that even some of your more distant relationships will begin to change as you see through strengths-colored glasses. You will discover that you suddenly understand and appreciate people whom you used to perceive as annoyances. Essentially, you will become more accepting of others.

Seeing Through Strengths-Colored Glasses Requires Courage

Seeing yourself and others through strengths-colored glasses — truly taking a strengths perspective — requires courage. Be forewarned: There may be some people in your life who don't want you to live out of your talents. Some of your friends and even your family members may be threatened by your talents. Some may envy your potential.

But instead of admitting their jealousy, they might be critical, poke fun, or otherwise try to make you feel that your talents are worthless. In the face of any level of ridicule, you must have the courage to be who you are and the courage to become the person you can be. Taking the strengths perspective demands the courage to be a person of integrity. You will quickly confront the issue of whether you are fully using your talents. It takes real courage to ask yourself, "Am I fully developing my talents into strengths?" And it takes even more courage to ask, "Am I fully applying my strengths?"

Through Strengths-Colored Glasses, You Will See Injustices Much More Clearly

One final aspect of the revolutionary nature of the strengths perspective is this: You will likely become less tolerant of institutional practices and traditions that demean people's unique natures. You will likely become sensitive to the practices and traditions that prevent people from knowing and realizing their talents. You may be particularly agitated when you observe institutions, organizations, groups, or interactions that demean people or that try to convince people that they have no talents.

Bear this in mind: When, through your strengths-colored glasses, you see injustices and abuses that prevent people from recognizing their talents and living through them, you will likely become a revolutionary force in bringing out the best that is within everyone.

Chapter V

Insights Into Strengths Development

As you have learned, a strength is the ability to provide consistent, near-perfect performance in a given activity. You've also learned that to build a strength, you first identify a dominant talent, then refine it with knowledge and skill.

But why would you *want* to build a strength? There are two big reasons you should develop your talents into strengths.

1. Your achievements depend on it.
2. Your personal fulfillment depends on it.

Those are two very good reasons, don't you think?

You cannot achieve excellence unless (a) you possess the talents that an achievement requires, (b) you develop those talents into strengths, and (c) you apply those strengths to the requirements of the achievement.

Also, there is a direct connection between your personal fulfillment and your talents. Just like achieving, your personal fulfillment stems from assuming personal responsibility for identifying and affirming your talents, then developing them into strengths and applying them as you pursue personally meaningful goals.

To this point, we have focused on helping you identify, affirm, and celebrate your talents. Now, it's time to focus on developing your talents into strengths.

Principles and Strategies for Developing Your Talents Into Strengths

Talents are like muscles. If you use them, they will help you achieve. Further, if you develop them, they will become stronger and even more capable of helping you achieve. In short, your achievements will rarely surpass the preparation and hard work you invest in developing and applying strengths.

Here are seven principles that you can use to govern the development of your talents into strengths. Specific suggestions follow each principle.

1. Know your talents.
Of course, before you can begin to develop your talents into strengths,

you must have somehow identified your talents. By taking StrengthsFinder and affirming the talents in your Signature Themes, you have done exactly that. As you continue reading and reflecting, you will refine that self-knowledge and solidify a foundation for developing your talents into strengths.

Here is a simple exercise that can help clarify your talents. Take a piece of paper and write down each of your five Signature Themes. Next, write down at least one talent that you believe you possess within each of those themes. Finally, write down an example of a time when you used each of those talents. If you can complete this exercise, you are building your awareness. This means that you have already begun to develop your talents into strengths!

2. You must value your talents and assume personal responsibility for developing them into strengths.

If you value your talents and assume personal responsibility for developing and applying them, you will invest the time, energy, and other necessary resources. If you don't value your talents, you won't make the investments that their development requires. At first you may not see the value of your talents. To correct this misperception, please think of the two or three most important things you have ever done. Or ponder your proudest moment, the time when you were at your best, doing what you do best.

Now, identify a talent that was at work in that situation. Next, imagine if you did not have this talent — what would have happened?

Now, from this perspective, do you value your talents enough to assume personal responsibility for developing them into strengths?

3. Talents best develop into strengths when inspired by a personal mission.

The philosopher Friedrich Nietzsche was quoted as saying, "He who has a 'why' to live for can bear almost any 'how.'"

What is the big "why" of your life? What are you ultimately trying to get done? What mission, purpose, or ultimate objective do you want to accomplish during your life?

These are the questions of "mission." A personal mission is the all-important task that you want to complete during your life. Your mission reflects what you hope will happen as a result of your actions. It is what brings meaning to your life.

Once you have formulated and clarified your personal mission, think about how your talents can help you fulfill it. Connecting your talents and mission is critical because your mission motivates you to develop your talents into strengths, and your strengths will empower you to fulfill your mission. Also, new ideas might emerge about how you can develop your talents into strengths while fulfilling your mission. Make sure you write down these ideas and follow through on them.

4. Healthy, caring relationships facilitate the development of strengths.

Having at least one healthy, caring relationship while developing your talents into strengths is enormously helpful. Here are some characteristics of the empowering relationships in which talents seem to best develop into strengths.

- There is mutual respect between you and the other person.
- You sense that he or she cares about you as a complete person.
- You can be open and honest with this person.
- You feel encouraged by being around this person.
- This person actively seeks to understand you.
- This person is a good listener.

In a healthy relationship that helps develop talents into strengths, certain events will likely occur.

- You will talk about your talents and where you see them already working in your life.
- You will express the specific talents you want to develop and how you plan to go about developing them.
- You will report on your efforts and experiences as you try to develop your talents.
- You will receive feedback based on your reported efforts and experiences as you try to develop your talents.
- You will work together to form expectations about your talents, how your strengths can be developed, and how you plan to apply

your strengths to produce specific achievements to levels of excellence.

In essence, you will be trying to form a relationship with someone who inspires you to greatness.

5. Reliving your successes helps develop your talents into strengths.

Every time you have succeeded, you have employed at least one of your talents. Consider those successes for a moment. Can you recognize specific talents that played roles in your successes? If you can, you are claiming ownership of those talents, and you are building confidence in them — and in the process, you are beginning to develop those talents into strengths.

To consider the roles your talents have played in your successes, try either talking or writing about them. As you try to capture in words the interplay between your talents and your successes, some powerful insights can occur.

6. Practice your talents.

As you use your talents over and over again, they will grow and become stronger. You will gain experience, and through that experience you will gain the knowledge and skills that are required for strength. Practice, practice, practice.

7. Teaching leads to learning.

To gain further understanding of talents and strengths, teach others about them. When you teach what you are learning, you are forced to learn it well enough to explain it to another person and answer his or her questions.

Now that you have gained a few insights into developing your talents into strengths, here's a challenge for you: Identify one specific area of your life where you want to achieve at a level of excellence. Next, identify a talent that you believe can contribute the most to excellence in this area. Finally, set a goal of developing that talent by using it at least twice as often as you are using it now.

Consider starting with one of your most dominant talents, possibly from your top Signature Theme. Beginning with the talent that brings you the greatest fulfillment would be a good idea, too.

To conclude this chapter, we would like you to consider another set of strategies. These particular strategies offer insights and action ideas for developing talents into strengths. Please locate and examine the strategies that are customized to your Signature Themes. As you examine them, try to select those that best fit the talents you feel you possess within your Signature Themes.

Developing Your Talents Into Strengths

Developing Your Achiever Talents Into Strengths

Your Achiever talents hold potential for strength, which is the key to excellence. These statements provide interesting insights and tips that can help you develop your talents into strengths.

☐ Select jobs in which you have the leeway to work as hard as you want and in which you are encouraged to measure your own productivity. You will feel challenged and alive in these environments.

☐ You do not require much motivation. Take advantage of your self-motivation by setting challenging goals. Set a higher goal every time you finish a project.

☐ Own the fact that you might work longer hours than most people and that you might not need as much sleep as many other people do.

☐ Choose to work with other hard workers. Share your goals with them so they can help you.

☐ Accept that you might be discontented even when you achieve.

☐ Focus your hard work on learning more.

☐ You want to have a purposeful, meaningful life. Make your plans using the criteria: "Is it important?" and "Will it be meaningful?"

☐ Even though you are full of energy, make sure you don't take on too many things at once. It is more important to achieve in a desired area than to simply be active.

Developing Your Activator Talents Into Strengths

Your Activator talents hold potential for strength, which is the key to excellence. These statements provide interesting insights and tips that can help you develop your talents into strengths.

- ☐ Seek work in which you can make your own decisions and act upon them.
- ☐ Take responsibility for your intensity by always asking for action when you are a part of a group.
- ☐ To avoid conflict later, ask your manager or teacher to judge you on measurable outcomes rather than your process. Your process might not always be popular, but your outcomes will likely be effective.
- ☐ Try to work only on action-oriented committees. Much committee work might prove very boring for you.
- ☐ Keep a log of accomplishments each day or week.
- ☐ Initiate action. Don't passively wait for others.
- ☐ Checklists are useful for you. Use them for time management by prioritizing and for stress relief when you have done what you needed to do.
- ☐ When insights or revelations occur, record them so you can act on them at the proper time.

Developing Your Adaptability Talents Into Strengths

Your Adaptability talents hold potential for strength, which is the key to excellence. These statements provide interesting insights and tips that can help you develop your talents into strengths.

☐ Seek roles in which success depends on responding to constantly changing circumstances. Consider career areas such as journalism, live television production, emergency healthcare, and customer service. In these types of roles, the best react the fastest and stay level headed.

☐ Fine-tune your responsiveness. For example, if your homework demands are unpredictable, learn how to adjust your schedule to accommodate when the pressure hits.

☐ When the pressure is on, help your friends find productive ways to relieve the pressure and therefore make progress. You can be the spark that "unfreezes" them.

☐ Cultivate your reputation as a calm and reassuring person when others become upset.

☐ Never apologize for your spontaneity. On the contrary, help others realize how many experiences might be missed if they don't seize the moment.

☐ You have outstanding abilities to adapt and adjust. Take things one at a time in your academic, social, and extracurricular activities.

☐ You tend to "take things as they come," and this is beautiful because you waste less time and energy.

☐ To others, things seem to just "fall into place" for you. This is good, but recognize that this isn't luck. It is because you have a talent for adjusting to changing circumstances.

Developing Your Analytical Talents Into Strengths

Your Analytical talents hold potential for strength, which is the key to excellence. These statements provide interesting insights and tips that can help you develop your talents into strengths.

- ☐ Choose work in which you are paid to analyze data, find patterns, or organize ideas. For example, you might excel at research (e.g., marketing, financial, medical), database management, editing, or risk management.

- ☐ Whatever your role, identify credible sources you can rely on. You are at your best when you have well-researched sources of information and numbers to support your logic. Determine the most helpful books, Web sites, or publications that can serve as references.

- ☐ Develop your skills in analysis by getting to know and share ideas with the outstanding analysts or experts who specialize in your area.

- ☐ Take an academic course that will stretch your Analytical talents. Specifically, study people whose logic you admire.

- ☐ Volunteer your Analytical talents. You can be particularly helpful to those who are struggling to organize large quantities of data or to bring structure to their ideas.

- ☐ Your exceptional eye for detail allows you to find things that are special or different. You see things others do not see.

- ☐ Look for the easiest way to approach a situation. Your talents allow you to simplify things and connect related concepts.

- ☐ Read as much as you can. You have a great capacity to bring information together.

Developing Your Arranger Talents Into Strengths

Your Arranger talents hold potential for strength, which is the key to excellence. These statements provide interesting insights and tips that can help you develop your talents into strengths.

☐ Seek complex, dynamic environments in which there are few routines.

☐ Offer your Arranger talents to help organize community service projects.

☐ Even the best arrangements or routines can be improved. Refine your talent by challenging yourself to find ways to make them more efficient.

☐ Study successful systems and arrangements to understand the configurations that work best. Make notes and apply the patterns you see to your own systems.

☐ Learn the talents of your friends, family, and coworkers. Help them figure out how they can match their talents to the tasks at hand.

☐ Organize a big event, a school dance perhaps, or coordinate a homecoming celebration or club project.

☐ Consider opportunities for supervising others. Develop systems to set people up for success based on their talents.

☐ Respect your ability to multitask and prioritize. These talents allow you to manage several projects at the same time.

Developing Your Belief Talents Into Strengths

Your Belief talents hold potential for strength, which is the key to excellence. These statements provide interesting insights and tips that can help you develop your talents into strengths.

- ☐ Clarify your values by thinking about one of your best days ever. How did your values contribute to the satisfaction that you received that day? How can you organize your life to repeat that day as often as possible?

- ☐ Don't be afraid to give voice to your values. This will help others know who you are and how to relate to you.

- ☐ Actively seek roles that fit your values. In particular, think about joining organizations that define their purpose by the contribution they make to society.

- ☐ Express your values outside of school. For example, volunteer at a hospital or run for an elected office.

- ☐ Actively seek friends who share your basic values.

- ☐ Adjust to new demands and situations, but maintain your values.

- ☐ Set your priorities and act accordingly: first things first.

- ☐ In your strongest area of belief, assume positions that promote and support that belief.

Developing Your Command Talents Into Strengths

Your Command talents hold potential for strength, which is the key to excellence. These statements provide interesting insights and tips that can help you develop your talents into strengths.

- ☐ Seek roles in which you will be asked to persuade others. Consider whether selling might be a good career for you.

- ☐ You don't shy away from confrontation. Practice the words, the tones, and the techniques that will turn your ability to confront into real persuasiveness.

- ☐ In your relationships, seize opportunities to speak plainly and directly about sensitive subjects. Your close friends may welcome and appreciate your unwillingness to hide from the truth.

- ☐ Help your friends and coworkers succeed by encouraging them to make commitments and follow through.

- ☐ Find a cause you believe in and support it. You might discover yourself at your best when defending a cause in the face of resistance.

- ☐ Ask the hard questions that help others face reality.

- ☐ Overcome obstacles. They can be motivating for you.

- ☐ Take control of situations you feel you can handle. If you fail, admit you were wrong, but don't give up (or blame others).

Developing Your Communication Talents Into Strengths

Your Communication talents hold potential for strength, which is the key to excellence. These statements provide interesting insights and tips that can help you develop your talents into strengths.

☐ You will likely do well in roles in which you are paid to capture people's attention. Your talents will probably flourish in teaching, sales, marketing, ministry, or the media.

☐ Practice telling stories you like by yourself. Listen to yourself actually saying the words.

☐ When you are presenting, listen closely to your audience. Watch their reactions to each part of your presentation. You will see that some parts prove especially engaging. After the presentation, take time to identify the parts that particularly caught the audience's attention. Draft your next presentation around these highlights.

☐ Articulate your goals. This helps to keep you motivated.

☐ Keep a log of stories that touch you emotionally. Tell them often.

☐ Speak up for your group.

☐ When others don't understand what is being said, rephrase it for them.

☐ Choose activities where you have an opportunity to talk.

Developing Your Competition Talents Into Strengths

Your Competition talents hold potential for strength, which is the key to excellence. These statements provide interesting insights and tips that can help you develop your talents into strengths.

☐ Select environments in which you can measure your achievements. You might never be able to discover how good you can be without competing.

☐ Take the time to celebrate your wins. In your world, there is no victory without celebration.

☐ Seek competitive friends.

☐ Try to turn ordinary tasks into competitive games. You will get more done this way.

☐ Avoid competitive situations in which results are not objectively evaluated or in which you have little chance of doing well.

☐ Compete against yourself. Top your last performance. Make your next paper better than the last, your grades higher than before.

☐ Winning motivates you. Strive to learn what it takes to win consistently.

☐ Choose to be in competitive events.

Developing Your Connectedness Talents Into Strengths

Your Connectedness talents hold potential for strength, which is the key to excellence. These statements provide interesting insights and tips that can help you develop your talents into strengths.

☐ You can become adept at helping other people see connection and purpose in everyday occurrences.

☐ Schedule time for meditation or contemplation. Reflect on how your religious beliefs affirm your sense of connection to others, how your sense of connection gives you stability through your faith in people, and the role of coincidences in your life.

☐ Make a list of the experiences that support your sense of connection.

☐ Join an organization that you feel puts Connectedness into practice.

☐ Help those around you cope with unpredictable and unexplainable events. In particular, you can help people find meaning in even sickness and death. Your perspective will bring comfort.

☐ Seek to understand the connectedness felt by others.

☐ Understand that you have a purpose in life. Discover it and fulfill it.

☐ Address your problems as they come up and meditate to find solutions.

Developing Your Consistency Talents Into Strengths

Your Consistency talents hold potential for strength, which is the key to excellence. These statements provide interesting insights and tips that can help you develop your talents into strengths.

☐ Make a list of rules of consistency by which you can live. These rules might be based on certain values or "non-negotiables" in your life. The clearer you make these rules, the more comfortable you will be with individuality within these boundaries.

☐ Seek roles in which you can be a force for leveling the playing field. You can be a leader in your community by providing disadvantaged people with the platform they need to show their true potential.

☐ Cultivate a reputation for pinpointing those who really deserve credit. Ensure that respect is always given to those who truly performed the work. You can become known as the conscience of your group.

☐ Find a role in which you can enforce compliance to a set of standards. Always be ready to challenge people who break the rules or "grease the wheels" to earn an advantage for themselves.

☐ Encourage consistency in club, team, and other group policies.

☐ Recognize excellent referees and umpires.

☐ Consider opportunities to judge according to established rules.

☐ Insist that rules apply the same to all people.

Developing Your Context Talents Into Strengths

Your Context talents hold potential for strength, which is the key to excellence. These statements provide interesting insights and tips that can help you develop your talents into strengths.

- ☐ Read historical novels, nonfiction, or biographies. You will discover many insights that will help you understand the present. You will think more clearly.

- ☐ Before project planning begins, encourage your classmates to study past projects. Help them appreciate the statement that "those who cannot remember the past are condemned to repeat it."

- ☐ If you are in a role that requires teaching others, build your lessons around case studies. You will enjoy the search for the appropriate case, and your students will learn from these precedents. Use your understanding of the past to help others map the future.

- ☐ Help your organization strengthen its culture via folklore. For example, collect symbols and stories that represent the best of the past, or suggest naming an award after a person who embodied the best of the past.

- ☐ When you are going to work with people, first, learn their past experiences.

- ☐ Consider being a historian or having a hobby of studying history.

- ☐ Make what has worked in the past a routine for the present.

- ☐ Help others understand how to make good decisions by looking at patterns in history.

Developing Your Deliberative Talents Into Strengths

Your Deliberative talents hold potential for strength, which is the key to excellence. These statements provide interesting insights and tips that can help you develop your talents into strengths.

☐ Consider work in which you can provide advice and counsel. You might be especially adept at legal work, crafting sound business deals, or ensuring compliance of regulations.

☐ During times of change, consider the advantages of being conservative in your decision-making. Be ready to explain these advantages to others when asked about your decisions.

☐ Have confidence in your own judgment. Do what you think is sensible, regardless of the impact on your popularity.

☐ Whatever your role, take responsibility for helping others think through their decisions. You will soon be sought as a valuable sounding board.

☐ Don't let anyone push you into revealing too much about yourself too soon. Check people out carefully before sharing confidential information. You naturally build friendships slowly, so take pride in your small circle of good friends.

☐ Take an active role in molding and shaping your own social atmosphere and academic environment in college.

☐ Be sure to set aside some time each day for yourself. It could be just five or 10 minutes. This time can be spent reflecting on the day, events, or anything that may be troubling you.

☐ Always think before you act. Apply this principle to all aspects of your life.

Developing Your Developer Talents Into Strengths

Your Developer talents hold potential for strength, which is the key to excellence. These statements provide interesting insights and tips that can help you develop your talents into strengths.

☐ Make a list of the people you have helped to learn and grow. Look at the list often, and remind yourself of the effect you have had on the world.

☐ Seek roles in which your primary responsibilities will be in facilitating growth. Teaching, coaching, or managing roles might prove especially satisfying for you.

☐ Notice when your friends learn and grow, and enhance their growth by sharing your specific observations.

☐ Make a list of the people you would like to help develop. Write what you would consider to be each person's strengths. Schedule time to meet with each of them regularly — even if for only 15 minutes — and make a point of discussing their goals and their strengths.

☐ Identify the mentor or mentors who recognized something special in you. Take the time to thank them for helping you develop, even if this means tracking down a former schoolteacher and sending him or her a letter.

☐ Make a plan to develop your own strengths based on a detailed understanding of your talents, knowledge, and skills.

☐ Discover talented young people who need help, and help them to develop.

☐ Find ways to help less fortunate people.

Developing Your Discipline Talents Into Strengths

Your Discipline talents hold potential for strength, which is the key to excellence. These statements provide interesting insights and tips that can help you develop your talents into strengths.

- ☐ Seek out roles and responsibilities where structure exists.

- ☐ Don't hesitate to check as often as necessary to ensure that things are right. You feel an urge to do it anyway, and soon enough others will come to expect it of you.

- ☐ Learn how to use a time management system. It will make you even more efficient and give you more confidence.

- ☐ Create routines that make you follow through systematically. Over time, people will come to appreciate this kind of rigorous predictability.

- ☐ Consider the best ways to discipline yourself. Apply these discipline strategies to efficiently achieve your goals.

- ☐ Try to maintain a structured lifestyle. Find a place for everything.

- ☐ Develop a calendar, and make things fit into it. Identify when and where to study and work.

- ☐ Maintain structure by keeping and regularly checking an organizer. Make daily "to do" lists to better organize your time and create some kind of routine. Check off what you do as you go through the day.

Developing Your Empathy Talents Into Strengths

Your Empathy talents hold potential for strength, which is the key to excellence. These statements provide interesting insights and tips that can help you develop your talents into strengths.

☐ Appreciate your gift for getting in touch with the thoughts and feelings of others.

☐ Practice naming the feelings you experience and those you observe in others. Then, help others name their feelings. People who can name their feelings seem to work better with other people.

☐ Build trust by letting others know that you know how they are feeling.

☐ Use your Empathy talents to help your friends relate to others in the group. Share your observations of others' feelings with them.

☐ Identify a friend who has strong Empathy, and check your observations with him or her.

☐ Sometimes it is important to be silent. You have the talent to let other people understand that you know how they are feeling, without even talking. Refine your nonverbal communication skills.

☐ Let others know that you can feel their pain.

☐ Understand and accept that it is okay to cry for people in pain and that your Empathy may lead you to do so.

Developing Your Focus Talents Into Strengths

Your Focus talents hold potential for strength, which is the key to excellence. These statements provide interesting insights and tips that can help you develop your talents into strengths.

☐ Take the time to write down your goals and refer to them often. You will feel more in control of your life.

☐ Seek roles in which you are asked to function independently. With your strong Focus theme, you will be able to stay on track with little supervision.

☐ Your greatest worth as a team member might be to help others set goals. At the end of each meeting, take responsibility for summarizing what was decided, defining when these decisions will be acted upon, and setting a date when the group will reconvene.

☐ Identify your role models. Write down in detail why you want to focus your career toward similar kinds of achievement.

☐ Think about what you want to be doing five years from now and how it relates to what you are learning and the skills you are presently developing. Think of this as a stepping stone toward your future endeavors.

☐ Allow your priorities to keep you grounded and lead you toward the right decisions and away from distractions.

☐ When attempting to solve a problem, consider your approach before taking action. Focus on the main objective.

☐ You may become discontented with anything you perceive as "busy work."

Developing Your Futuristic Talents Into Strengths

Your Futuristic talents hold potential for strength, which is the key to excellence. These statements provide interesting insights and tips that can help you develop your talents into strengths.

- ☐ Choose roles in which you can contribute your ideas about the future. For example, you might excel in entrepreneurial or start-up situations.

- ☐ Take time to think about the future. The more time you spend considering your ideas about the future, the more vivid your ideas will become. The more vivid your ideas, the more persuasive you will be.

- ☐ Seek audiences that appreciate your ideas for the future. They will expect you to make these ideas a reality, and these expectations will motivate you.

- ☐ Motivate your friends with goals that can be achieved in the future. For example, include some futuristic ideas in each of your group meetings, or write down your vision for the future and share it with your friends.

- ☐ Find a friend or colleague who possesses this theme. Set aside an hour a month for "future" discussions. Together, you can push each other to greater heights of creativity and vividness.

- ☐ Keep pictures, books, mental notes, or other reminders of what you are working toward.

- ☐ Visualize your future. Think about what you can do now to make that future better.

- ☐ Share your visions to evoke images of the future in the minds of peers.

Developing Your Harmony Talents Into Strengths

Your Harmony talents hold potential for strength, which is the key to excellence. These statements provide interesting insights and tips that can help you develop your talents into strengths.

☐ When working with others, stress the value of being agreeable.

☐ Build a network of people with differing perspectives. Rely on these people when you need expertise. Your openness to these differing perspectives will help you learn.

☐ Accept the responsibilities of being a good team member. Your willingness to adjust and your tolerance for differing views can become significant strengths.

☐ When two people are arguing, ask others in the group to share their thoughts. By increasing the number of voices in the conversation, you are more likely to find areas where all parties can agree. You can draw people together.

☐ Avoid roles that will lead you to confront people on a daily basis. Sales roles based on "cold calls" or roles in highly competitive workplaces, for example, may frustrate or upset you.

☐ Use your agreeableness to promote positive attitudes in others.

☐ Practice finding what is common among people.

☐ Challenge groups to discover areas of agreement.

Developing Your Ideation Talents Into Strengths

Your Ideation talents hold potential for strength, which is the key to excellence. These statements provide interesting insights and tips that can help you develop your talents into strengths.

☐ Find work in which you will be given credit for your ideas, such as marketing, advertising, journalism, design, or new product development.

☐ You get bored quickly, so make small changes in your school, work, or home life to keep yourself stimulated and focused. Challenge yourself with mental games or small goals related to the task at hand.

☐ Seek brainstorming sessions. With your abundance of ideas, you will make these sessions more exciting and more productive.

☐ Discuss your ideas with other people. Their responses will help you keep refining your ideas.

☐ When an idea comes to you, write it down and list the actions you can take to make it happen.

☐ Create ways to get the "impossible" done. Come up with creative solutions to problems.

☐ Value your ideas. Because they come to you so easily, you might not recognize how valuable they could be to others.

☐ Make time to think. Ideas energize you.

Developing Your Includer Talents Into Strengths

Your Includer talents hold potential for strength, which is the key to excellence. These statements provide interesting insights and tips that can help you develop your talents into strengths.

- ☐ Choose roles in which you are continuously working and interacting with people. You will enjoy the challenge of making everyone feel important.

- ☐ Consider roles in which you are responsible for representing voices that are not normally heard. You will derive a great deal of satisfaction from being their representative.

- ☐ Look for opportunities to bring together people of diverse cultures and backgrounds. You can be a leader in this area.

- ☐ Help those who are new to a group get to know other people. You will be adept at quickly making people feel accepted and involved.

- ☐ Bring outsiders in by recognizing their talents and asking them to contribute to the group through those talents.

- ☐ Talk to people who seem to feel left out.

- ☐ Invite "loners" to sit beside you in class.

- ☐ Speak up for the importance of everyone's feelings being accepted.

Developing Your Individualization Talents Into Strengths

Your Individualization talents hold potential for strength, which is the key to excellence. These statements provide interesting insights and tips that can help you develop your talents into strengths.

☐ Select a vocation in which your Individualization theme can be appreciated and used, such as counseling, supervising, teaching, writing human-interest articles, or selling.

☐ Become an expert in describing your own strengths and style. For example, answer questions such as these: What is the best praise you ever received? How often do you like to check in with your teachers? What is your best method for building relationships? How do you learn best?

☐ Help your family and friends plan their future by helping them define their strengths. Then, design a future based on those strengths.

☐ Make your family and friends aware of each person's unique needs. Soon people will look to you to explain other people's motivations and actions.

☐ Study successful people to discover the uniqueness that made them successful.

☐ Consider that you might be able to write a novel.

☐ Actively seek one-to-one relationships. This will give you the greatest opportunity to use and develop your Individualization talents.

☐ Choose opportunities that use your gift for figuring out how different people work together productively.

Developing Your Input Talents Into Strengths

Your Input talents hold potential for strength, which is the key to excellence. These statements provide interesting insights and tips that can help you develop your talents into strengths.

- ☐ Look for jobs in which you are charged with acquiring new information each day, such as teaching, research, or journalism.

- ☐ Identify your areas of specialization, and actively seek more information about them.

- ☐ Schedule time to read books and articles that stimulate you.

- ☐ Deliberately increase your vocabulary. Collect new words, and learn the meaning of each word.

- ☐ You might enjoy reading the dictionary and the encyclopedia. This might seem strange to some people, but for someone like you it is a good way to strengthen your self-concept.

- ☐ Devise a system to store and easily locate information. This can be as simple as a file for all the articles you have clipped or as sophisticated as a computer database.

- ☐ Identify situations in which you can share the information you have collected with other people.

- ☐ Seek information on the Web, in bookstores, or in libraries whenever possible.

Developing Your Intellection Talents Into Strengths

Your Intellection talents hold potential for strength, which is the key to excellence. These statements provide interesting insights and tips that can help you develop your talents into strengths.

- ☐ Consider beginning or continuing your studies in philosophy, literature, or psychology. You will enjoy subjects that stimulate your thinking.

- ☐ Although you are a natural thinker, make a point to schedule time for thinking. Use this time to muse, reflect, and reenergize.

- ☐ List your ideas in a log or a diary. These ideas will serve as grist for your mental mill, and they might yield valuable insights.

- ☐ Take time to write. Writing might be the best way to crystallize and integrate your thoughts.

- ☐ Find people who like to talk about the same issues you do. Organize a discussion group that addresses subjects of interest to you.

- ☐ Build relationships with people you consider to be "big thinkers." Their example will inspire you to focus your own thinking.

- ☐ Consider the circumstances in which you do your best thinking. Do you prefer to be alone or with others? Do you prefer a quiet environment or a noisy one? Is there a specific place where you do your best thinking?

- ☐ You have a talent for making "mind movies" that you can enjoy by yourself.

Developing Your Learner Talents Into Strengths

Your Learner talents hold potential for strength, which is the key to excellence. These statements provide interesting insights and tips that can help you develop your talents into strengths.

☐ Choose a career in a field with constantly changing technologies or regulations. You will be energized by the challenge of keeping up.

☐ Because you are not threatened by unfamiliar information, you might excel in a consulting role in which you are paid to go into new situations and pick up new competencies or languages very quickly.

☐ Refine how you learn. You might learn best by teaching. If so, seek out opportunities to present to others. You might learn best through quiet reflection. If so, schedule this quiet time.

☐ Find ways to track the progress of your learning. If there are distinct levels or stages of learning within a discipline or skill, celebrate your progression from one level to the next. If no such levels exist, create them for yourself (for example, read five books on the subject or make three presentations on the subject).

☐ Join an organization that prides itself on being a learning organization.

☐ Consider becoming a professor or researcher.

☐ Learning is meaningful to you. Keep the mentality that you are never done learning, not even when school is over. You are a lifelong learner.

☐ View learning as a way of life, a way to improve, a way to develop, and a privilege.

Developing Your Maximizer Talents Into Strengths

Your Maximizer talents hold potential for strength, which is the key to excellence. These statements provide interesting insights and tips that can help you develop your talents into strengths.

☐ Seek roles in which you help other people succeed. In coaching, managing, mentoring, or teaching roles, your focus on talents will prove particularly beneficial. For example, because most people find it difficult to describe what they do best, start by arming them with vivid descriptions.

☐ Devise ways to measure your performance and the performances of your friends. The best way to identify talent is to look for sustained levels of excellent performance.

☐ To maximize most effectively, focus on your greatest talents, as they are your best opportunities for strengths. Acquire and develop related skills. Gain relevant knowledge. Keep working toward mastery in a your areas of greatest potential.

☐ Develop a plan to use your talents outside of school. Consider how they relate your mission in life and how they might benefit your family or the community.

☐ Study success. Spend time with people who have developed their talents into strengths. The more you understand how strengths lead to success, the more likely you will be to create success in your own life.

☐ Stay aware of the strengths you want to develop and of the talents they require.

☐ Even talented Maximizers can be tempted to focus on weaknesses. Avoid this temptation. Maximize your own talents by intentionally focusing on potential strength.

☐ Know that discovering talents and building strengths are lifelong processes. Every phase and aspect of your life will offer new opportunities for maximization.

Developing Your Positivity Talents Into Strengths

Your Positivity talents hold potential for strength, which is the key to excellence. These statements provide interesting insights and tips that can help you develop your talents into strengths.

☐ You will excel in roles in which you are paid to highlight the positive. A teaching role, a sales role, an entrepreneurial role, or a leadership role call for and stretch your talents.

☐ You tend to be more enthusiastic and energetic than most people. When others become discouraged or are reluctant to take risks, your attitude will provide the motivation to keep them moving. Over time, others will start to look to you for this "lift."

☐ Help others see the things that are going well for them. You can keep their eyes on the positive.

☐ Because people will rely on you to help them rise above their daily frustrations, arm yourself with good stories, jokes, and sayings. Never underestimate the effect that you can have on people.

☐ Plan highlight activities for your friends. For example, find ways to turn small achievements into events, plan regular celebrations that others can look forward to, or capitalize on the year's holidays and festivals.

☐ When facing adversity, focus on the positive aspects of life.

☐ Engage in possibility thinking.

☐ Own your optimism.

Developing Your Relator Talents Into Strengths

Your Relator talents hold potential for strength, which is the key to excellence. These statements provide interesting insights and tips that can help you develop your talents into strengths.

- ☐ Find a workplace in which friendships are encouraged. You may not do well in an overly formal organization. In a job interview, ask about work styles and company culture.

- ☐ Listen to people with unconditional regard.

- ☐ Learn as much as you can about the people you meet. You like knowing about people, and other people like being known. You will be a catalyst for trusting relationships.

- ☐ Your noticeable interest in character and personality — rather than status or job title — can serve as a model for others.

- ☐ Let your caring show. For example, find people in your school to mentor, help your friends get to know each other better, or extend your relationships beyond the classroom.

- ☐ No matter how busy you are, stay in contact with your friends. They are your fuel.

- ☐ Support your friends at emotional and ceremonial times (i.e., weddings, graduations, funerals).

- ☐ Enjoy doing things with people as well as for them.

Developing Your Responsibility Talents Into Strengths

Your Responsibility talents hold potential for strength, which is the key to excellence. These statements provide interesting insights and tips that can help you develop your talents into strengths.

☐ Emphasize your sense of responsibility when job hunting. During interviews, describe your desire to be held fully accountable for the success or failure of projects, your intense dislike of unfinished work, and your need to "make it right" if a commitment is not met.

☐ Keep volunteering for more responsibility than your experience seems to warrant. You thrive on responsibility and can deal with it very effectively.

☐ Align yourself with others who share your sense of responsibility. You will enjoy this sense of complete team integrity.

☐ Tell your parents and teachers that you work best when given the independence to follow through on your commitments. Tell them that you don't need to check in during a project, just at the end. You can be trusted to get it done.

☐ You may enjoy leading study groups.

☐ Ask for the goals of an assignment, then figure out how you can best achieve the goals.

☐ In your own efforts to be responsible, don't assume that others are irresponsible. By doing so, you would risk depriving them of the opportunity to take responsibility.

☐ Keep a checklist of things to do, and check off each item as you complete it. You will derive motivation and satisfaction from doing so.

Developing Your Restorative Talents Into Strengths

Your Restorative talents hold potential for strength, which is the key to excellence. These statements provide interesting insights and tips that can help you develop your talents into strengths.

☐ Seek roles in which you are paid to solve problems. You might particularly enjoy medicine, consulting, computer programming, or customer service, in which your success depends on your ability to restore and resolve.

☐ Study your chosen subject closely to become adept at identifying what causes certain problems to recur. This sort of expertise will lead you to the solution much faster.

☐ In your relationships, don't be afraid to let others know that you enjoy fixing problems. It comes naturally to you, but many people shy away from problems. You can help.

☐ Think about ways you can improve your skills and knowledge. Identify courses you can take to fill gaps in your knowledge.

☐ Make a list of ways that you could help people who are disadvantaged, such as volunteering in your community or fund raising.

☐ Don't ignore your weaknesses; manage them.

☐ Volunteer to be the "fix it" person in your favorite group.

☐ If you feel lacking in a certain area, focus on your strengths to define the obstacle, and then overcome it.

Developing Your Self-Assurance Talents Into Strengths

Your Self-Assurance talents hold potential for strength, which is the key to excellence. These statements provide interesting insights and tips that can help you develop your talents into strengths.

- ☐ Seek start-up situations for which no rulebook exists. You will be at your best when you are asked to make many decisions.

- ☐ Seek roles in which you are charged with persuading people to see your point of view. Your Self-Assurance, especially when combined with strong Command or Activator themes, can create an extremely persuasive combination. Therefore, leadership, sales, legal, or entrepreneurial roles might be appropriate.

- ☐ Appeal to your internal guidance system to determine appropriate actions. Trust your instincts.

- ☐ Let your self-confidence show. It will be reinforcing to your friends.

- ☐ Help others find the positives in your certainty. For example, when you have decided what you are going to do, they can trust that you will do it.

- ☐ You have a deep belief that achievement is always possible because you have an inherent ability to succeed. This belief will be a constant source of energy for you.

- ☐ Trust your inner sense of guidance and direction when it comes to large and small issues. While it is important to consult and gain information on class selection, choosing a major, deciding on an approach to a project, and forming a thesis or argument, when making your final decision, trust your inner compass.

- ☐ Your Self-Assurance can provide the persistence required to reach challenging goals. Use your Self-Assurance to think big and achieve big.

Developing Your Significance Talents Into Strengths

Your Significance talents hold potential for strength, which is the key to excellence. These statements provide interesting insights and tips that can help you develop your talents into strengths.

☐ Choose jobs or positions in which you can determine your own tasks and actions. You will enjoy the exposure that comes with independence.

☐ Your reputation is important to you, so decide what you want it to be, and tend to it in the smallest detail. Identify and earn a designation that will add to your credibility, write an article that will give you visibility, or volunteer to speak in front of a group that will admire your achievements.

☐ Make a list of the goals, achievements, and qualifications you crave, and post them where you will see them every day. Use this list to inspire yourself.

☐ Identify your best moment of recognition or praise. What was it for? Who gave it to you? Who was the audience? What do you have to do to recreate that moment?

☐ Share your dreams and goals with your family or closest friends. Their expectations for you will keep you reaching for those dreams and goals.

☐ Attaining a degree or certification might solidify a role and status in your community.

☐ Voice your opinions, and put yourself in positions where your opinions can be heard and appreciated.

☐ Take actions that will provide the recognition you crave.

Developing Your Strategic Talents Into Strengths

Your Strategic talents hold potential for strength, which is the key to excellence. These statements provide interesting insights and tips that can help you develop your talents into strengths.

☐ Make full use of your Strategic talents by scheduling time to carefully think about a goal you want to achieve and the paths you might take to reach it. Remember that time to contemplate is essential to strategic thinking.

☐ You can see potential repercussions more clearly than others. Use your Strategic talents to not only point out possible problems, but to provide helpful alternatives.

☐ Talk with others about the alternative directions you see. Detailed conversations like this can help you become even better at anticipating.

☐ Even though you might not be able to rationally explain your intuitions, you are naturally talented at anticipating outcomes.

☐ Trust your insights. When the time comes, seize the moment and state your strategy with confidence.

☐ Find a group that you think does important work and contribute your strategic thinking. You can be a leader with your ideas.

☐ Use your talents to understand and to work beyond barriers. You see many alternatives. Choose one.

☐ Brainstorm for solutions when approaching a problem. Ask, "What if?" Write down all possible ways of approaching the problem, then think about the consequences of each, and decide which would be the most effective and efficient solution.

Developing Your Woo Talents Into Strengths

Your Woo talents hold potential for strength, which is the key to excellence. These statements provide interesting insights and tips that can help you develop your talents into strengths.

☐ Choose a job in which you can interact with many people over the course of a day.

☐ Build the network of people who know you. Tend to it by checking in with each person at least once a month.

☐ Join local organizations, volunteer for committees, and find out how to get on the social lists of the influential people where you live.

☐ Learn the names of as many people as you can. Build a file of the people you know, and add names as you become acquainted. Include a snippet of personal information, such as a birthday, favorite color, hobby, or favorite sports team.

☐ Consider running for an elected office. You are a natural campaigner. Understand, however, that you might prefer the campaigning more than holding the office.

☐ Recognize that your ability to get people to like you is very valuable. Don't be afraid to use it to make things happen.

☐ In social situations, take responsibility for helping put more reserved people at ease.

☐ Practice ways to charm and engage others. For example, research people before you meet them so you can find some common ground.

Chapter VI

CONSIDERING STRENGTHS WHEN PLANNING YOUR EDUCATION

Personal excellence is the objective to keep in mind when planning an education. Accordingly, each and every step in the planning process should lead to higher and higher levels of personal excellence.

The essence of planning every aspect of an education that will lead to personal excellence, right down to each course you select, lies in answering one question:

Will it help you become all that you have the talent and opportunity to be?

To help you answer this question in planning your education, we will share the lessons we have learned about excellence from studying great learners, educators, and leaders.

Five Facts That Great Learners, Educators, and Leaders Know About Excellence

1. **Our talents hold the key to excellence.**

Many people mistakenly think that their greatest potential for growth is in their weakness. But this is not true. We grow and develop most when we are working on and working with our talents and strengths. Our greatest potential for growth toward excellence is found in our talents and strengths.

2. **Simply having talents or strengths isn't enough to produce excellence. Talents must be developed into strengths, and strengths must be applied. This requires practice and hard work.**

Some people think that merely possessing talents and strengths ensures easy achievement of excellence. But great learners, educators, and leaders know that this is pure myth. As in any area of life, achieving excellence in education requires meticulous, painstaking preparation and hard work.

3. **Excellence requires that you have a clear idea about what excellence is, what it looks like, and what is required to reach it.**

To achieve excellence, you must simply study excellence. This means first having in mind a clear image of what excellence looks like. Then, you must study the behavior patterns necessary to produce excellence.

For example, as a student, you should know what an excellent paper or essay reads like in order to write one. The image of excellence must be crystal clear.

One "straight A" college student developed a unique way of forming such a mental image of excellence that helped him write papers. First, he reasoned that if an article or a book gets published, at least one person must think it's excellent. But he further reasoned that different people might have varying ideas about excellence. So, this young man went to the library and found book reviews on each of the books he was assigned in his classes.

By reading book reviews on the books in his classes, he was able to form a mental image of what was, and what was not, excellent about a particular book. This not only produced a mental image of what excellence looks like, but it also gave him ideas about how to critically analyze the materials presented in his classes. Armed with this information and the mental images that had emerged, this young man was prepared to write papers and essay examinations on the texts assigned in his courses.

4. Focusing on one area of talent at a time is the best route to excellence.

There is a danger in diffusing your attention and effort by focusing on too many things at once. Taking one area of talent at a time and developing it to the maximum moves you to excellence most efficiently. Once a person has reached excellence in one area, a framework for and an understanding of excellence in other areas is likely to emerge. Your own questioning mind sets a direction and can fuel your pursuit of excellence. Your curiosities reveal where you want to grow, develop, and learn more. This provides a focus for where you may want to be excellent. Therefore, let your questioning mind tell you where you are most motivated to learn, grow, and develop.

5. It is also important to realize that many talents — all working together and strategically applied — are necessary to produce excellence.

Achieving excellence isn't easy. Quite often, a strength is rooted in not just one talent, but two, three, or even more. This is one of the reasons why reaching levels of excellence takes considerable time and practice.

Think about the meaning of your talents in combination. Begin by focusing on your two most powerful Signature Themes. How do your talents within these themes interact with one another? What does that interaction tend to produce? Now, consider your talents in your third Signature Theme. How do your talents in these three themes interact and influence one another?

Think about what you want to get out of college. In essence, what are your desired outcomes? Consider the ways that you want to develop as a person.

Think about the skills you want to develop. For example, do you want to hone your writing, mathematical, and/or problem-solving skills? Perhaps you are most interested in developing your thinking skills. Consider the knowledge you want to gain. In what areas do you want to be more knowledgeable than you are today? What information, insights, and understandings will you need for the future?

Now, think about the matter of awareness. Perhaps you would like to become more aware of your own culture and the meanings of various traditions. Perhaps you want to become aware of various modes of artistic expression or understand the nature of science.

Consider career outcomes. Do you hope that college will help you identify a career? Do you expect your college experience to prepare you for a career? If so, what do you need to learn while in college to be effective in your career?

On an entirely different level, perhaps you look at the college experience as a time to clarify or affirm your values. Maybe you look at college as a time to set a direction for your life and make a group of commitments regarding yourself and your future.

Whatever the case, the first focus of planning a college education should be on your desired outcomes. Clearly, those outcomes are directly related to the decisions you make not only before you begin college, but also while you're in college. Each term, you will make a group of decisions regarding what classes you will sign up for and who your professors will be. We urge you to make informed decisions about classes and professors, as they will have a direct impact on your outcomes.

Last, but not least, consider graduation requirements, the structure of the degree, and requirements you may need to fulfill to enter a particular career or graduate-school program.

Questions to Help Your Educational Planning

Academic advisors are marvelous college resources. Staff and advising faculty offer a great deal to your educational planning process.

To help you prepare for meeting with your advisor and to help you make wise involvement decisions, we have listed several questions for your thoughtful reflections.

1. Self-Assessment of Talents

- Which of your Signature Themes describe you best?

- Which of your Signature Themes hold the talents you use most frequently?

- In which of your Signature Themes are your talents most highly developed?

- Which talents do you most want to develop in college?

2. Motivations, Dreams, and Desires About College

- What are you hoping will happen while you are in college?

- What do you want to be able to do as a result of going to college?

- Imagine that you have graduated from college and you feel great. What would make you feel so great about your experience?

- Which of your talents do you believe will be most instrumental in helping you fulfill your dreams and desires for college?

- Which of your talents will you be planning to develop through classes and extracurricular activities?

- What images come to your mind when you think about fully developing your talents into strengths?

3. Self-Assessments of Intellectual Interest and Curiosities

- What do you seem to learn with the greatest ease?

- What have your teachers complimented you about?

- What do you have a burning desire to know and understand?

4. Vocational, Career, and Graduate School Aspirations

- To date, what experiences have been your most fulfilling?
- Which careers seem most interesting and attractive to you?
- In what career would you be able to best use your talents and strengths?
- Given your general career interests and vocation, what types of graduate-school training will you need?
- Which courses and college opportunities can help you best prepare for your vocation, career, and graduate school?

5. Time and Energy Demands

- What are your family responsibilities, and how much time will they require each week?
- How many hours per week must you work to meet your financial responsibilities?
- To achieve highly in each of your classes, how much time will be required each week?
- Which of your talents and strengths can you count on to make you time- and energy-efficient?

6. Self-Assessment of Academic Abilities

- In what areas do you feel that you have the greatest academic abilities?
- On what types of tests do you score highest?
- What has been your favorite type of assignment?
- What subjects do you most enjoy studying ?
- How have your talents and strengths helped you succeed in the past?
- In which academic tasks do you best apply your talents and strengths?
- In which academic tasks would you like to discover how to better apply your talents and strengths?

7. Degree Structure and Requirements

- What courses must you take to graduate?

- Where do you have flexibility in fulfilling graduation requirements?

- What are the graduate-school entrance requirements for the programs you are considering?

- What classes will best prepare you to enter the career or graduate schools you are considering?

Final Considerations in Planning Your Education

Your answers to the previous questions will help you create a plan to achieve your desired educational outcomes — but there is certainly more to consider.

Equally important is the issue of timing. When should you take certain college classes? When should you become involved in the various college programs, services, activities, and resources that are available?

In answering each of these questions, and in making your plan for education a reality, you should make strengths development "priority one." Doing so will help you gain confidence, build your motivation, heighten your sense of direction, and lead you to an enjoyable experience in taking on the many challenges and opportunities offered by the college experience.

Chapter VII

DEVELOPING ACADEMIC AND LEADERSHIP STRENGTHS IN COLLEGE

You have considered the importance of talents and strengths in planning your education to achieve personal excellence. Now, it is time to plot out how to develop your talents into strengths while you are in college, both in general and in leadership roles.

Four Tips for Developing Strengths in College

Your overall academic experience can be greatly enhanced by the perspective and direction you take in setting goals and making key decisions. Consider these four suggestions.

1. **Define college success in terms of developing your talents into strengths.**

If you are going to assume responsibility for your college experience, you must come to grips with defining success for yourself.

So, what is the best outcome of college that you can imagine? Most people would say getting a 4.0 GPA, graduating Magna Cum Laude, getting a well-paying job, or gaining admission to medical school, law school, or some other graduate or professional school. These are good, but your considerations should go beyond your college years. Defining college success in terms of developing your talents into strengths emphasizes *building yourself into a person of excellence.*

2. **Select classes on the basis of your talents and strengths.**

Considering your talents is particularly important as you select classes for the early portion of your college education. In these early years, it is especially important to build your confidence and to develop your talents into strengths. Far too many students who enroll in college never graduate, and many of those who drop out do so in the first year. Why? Quite frequently, the reason is that they have selected classes that do not suit their talents. As a result, they do not experience the success they expected, and then they become frustrated and disillusioned and eventually give up.

Be sure to continue to apply the strengths-based approach during the rest of your college career. This means that *each time* you select your classes, ask yourself two questions: (1) Which of my talents will I be able to apply in this class? and (2) Which of my talents will I be able to develop into strengths in this class? If you don't know the answer to either of these questions, get more information about the classes you are considering. If you have to say "none" to both questions, you must ask yourself why you are enrolling in the class in the first place.

These comments may be controversial, so let's be clear. We are not being anti-liberal arts, nor are we trying to undermine the need for all students to have certain basic skills. We are certainly not trying to limit students' exploration of new fields.

What we oppose is educational practices that give students placement tests to find out what students *can't do* or *don't know* — and then force them to focus first on where they struggle before they can learn about their talents.

3. Consider your talents when selecting extracurricular activities.

To gain maximum benefits from college, think about college as a total experience in which you *purposely become as deeply involved as possible.* This means making college the focal point of your life. Becoming personally involved might include studying on campus, forming study groups, meeting with professors, and making use of campus programs and services. If possible, live on campus or near campus, and live with other students, or at least form close relationships with people from college.

As you make decisions about extracurricular involvement, seek opportunities to develop your talents into strengths. For example, form relationships with professors and students who share your talents. Become involved in clubs and organizations that provide opportunities for you to use or develop strengths.

4. Choose your college jobs by considering the opportunities they provide to develop your talents into strengths.

Most college students must work in order to make ends meet. That is a reality, but it is also true that employment during college presents another opportunity to develop your talents into strengths. Therefore, carefully consider where you'll be employed and what type of work you'll do. The most ideal situation would be (1) to work on campus so you can increase your involvement, and (2) to work in a job where you can use and develop at least one of your talents into a strength. That way, you will be doing more than just earning money.

Developing Leadership Strengths in College

For many people, college is a stepping-stone to careers in which they will be leaders. They might hope to lead in a classroom, a courtroom, a corporation, a community, a hospital, an agency, a ministry, or their own business. Also, many college graduates will move into supervisory roles. Both of these facts point to the importance of learning about effective leadership.

All of the talents in the themes measured by StrengthsFinder can be applied to leadership roles and responsibilities. Therefore, if you assume any leadership roles in college, you will have opportunities to develop your talents into strengths.

Take mentoring, for example. Often, when a college student is mentored by a professor or staff member on campus, that student's intellectual and personal development increases significantly. Even fellow students, especially those who are a year or two ahead of you, can be very helpful as mentors. You would probably find it very beneficial to have a peer with whom you can continually reflect on your college experience.

But *being* a mentor is just as important as *having* a mentor. Even while you are being mentored, try to serve as a mentor to someone else. For example, especially if you have been in college two or more years, you could mentor an entering freshman. You could also help other students prepare for exams in courses in which you are knowledgeable.

Both having a mentor and being a mentor enrich your college experience in many ways. If you truly want to turn your talents into strengths, you must seek out people to help you — and find people who would benefit from what you have learned.

The college experience provides a magnificent opportunity to develop your leadership talents into strengths. The key is to be intentional. Talents within each and every one of your Signature Themes can be applied in college, and many can be applied in multiple leadership functions. Look for every opportunity to develop and apply your strengths for leadership.

In our work with thousands of college students, we have identified several ways in which you can intentionally develop your leadership strengths in college. We present these suggestions to stimulate your thinking. There are certainly many more ways to use the college experience to build your leadership strengths. Let your imagination devise the approach and the activities that are best for you.

1. Leadership development and the college experience in general

Pay particular attention to when and how you influence others and how you are able to rally others to make changes. Conversely, note when and how others influence you and rally you to make changes.

2. Leadership development and the classroom experience

Classes and the work of instructors in the classroom provide wonderful opportunities to learn about leadership. Since learning always involves changing — and since leadership is designed to produce measurable change — you will want to note when and how instructors influence students to change. Here are some questions that will stimulate your thinking as you learn about leadership from observing and reflecting on the work of educators as leaders.

- What is the difference between effective and ineffective instructors?
- What strengths do the best instructors seem to have?
- How do the best instructors interact with students?
- How do the best instructors organize lessons and classroom activities?
- How do the most effective instructors persuade others?
- How do effective instructors use their strengths when they teach and interact with students?
- Which strengths do you have in common with the most effective instructors?

3. Leadership development and class selection

Almost all the classes in a field of study can provide valuable insights for the learner who intentionally wants to develop leadership strengths. Here are some examples.

- any classes in communication studies or speech
- any classes in leadership studies or management
- almost all classes in sociology or social psychology
- most classes in organizational development, organizational psychology, and community development

- humanities classes that focus on rhetoric and persuasion
- philosophy classes in argumentation and logical reasoning
- mathematical reasoning and patterns in scientific problem-solving classes
- most classes in political science
- many classes in cultural anthropology
- many classes in ethnic and cross-cultural studies
- history and other social science classes that focus on the dynamics of change and/or the influence of particular leaders in the change process

4. Leadership development in class assignments and independent studies

Make class assignments work for you by applying them to the study of leaders and leadership. We recommend you focus your studies on the best leaders and the reasons for their outstanding performances. You may be able to do library research and study historical or current leaders. Or, conduct your own investigations of the best leaders you know or the best in a particular field. As you study, here are some questions to consider.

- What is it that makes these leaders so effective?
- What strengths do they have?
- In what environment and with what groups of people do leaders with certain strengths seem to be most effective?

5. Leadership development in athletics

On the most basic level, athletics can help you understand a lot about leadership and the concept of talents and strengths. You also learn about how you need different types of talent to play different kinds of sports and positions. Then, there is the whole challenge of turning talents into strengths and the attitudes that are involved.

Additional insights about leadership can be gained from asking the following questions about sports and athletic competition.

- What makes a great coach?
- How do effective coaches work with their players?

- What are effective coaches doing during practice and during a game?

- What are the most important elements of preparation?

- What are the most important things to do and not do during training?

- What is the best way to learn a new approach, a new play, or new moves?

- What is involved in changing old habits and developing new ones?

- What are the best ways to formulate goals?

- How can you best develop a "team" and "team spirit"?

- How can you best deal with discouragements, injuries, and setbacks?

- What are the most effective ways to maintain motivation?

6. Leadership development through internships and experiential education opportunities

Most colleges and universities offer internships in which you can work with professionals in a given field. These provide up-close and personal looks at how leadership works in real life. Even if the internship isn't the most positive experience, you can learn what not to do when you are a leader. Also, you may have opportunities to perform several other leadership functions through your internship or experiential education opportunity.

7. Leadership development in study groups

As you work with other students in study groups, use your various strengths to help yourself and others learn. For example, an effective leader helps others use their strengths to help the group function better and to move toward a desired goal. Likewise, consider the strengths of other members of your study group, and try to allocate the tasks of the study group according to those strengths.

As you use study groups to develop leadership strengths, look for every opportunity to help other people learn more about their talents and strengths. In the process, you will be learning more about your own.

8. Leadership development through student organizations

Student clubs, organizations, and service projects provide some of the best leadership development opportunities available on campus. The opportunities are numerous as there are many leadership roles to be filled, and students fill nearly all of them. But this also presents a massive challenge because students have multiple commitments and competing priorities, and their work in student organizations is almost exclusively unpaid. However, students who meet the challenge of providing appropriate attention to each of their responsibilities receive excellent opportunities to develop leadership strengths.

9. Leadership development through employment and work experience

Nearly every college student works to pay some or all of his or her college and living expenses. But rather than considering employment as only a job for earning money, try to make it a learning experience through which you can develop leadership strengths.

Managing others can be one of the most important aspects of leadership. From the strengths perspective, managers will be most effective if they capitalize on their strengths and consciously use them as they manage others.

The best way to manage someone takes into account the strengths of both the manager and those who are managed. A best-selling book from The Gallup Organization, *Now, Discover Your Strengths*, offers specific strategies for how a manager can use his or her strengths to best manage others. The same book describes how to take into account the individual strengths of those who are being managed.

Armed with the knowledge contained in *Now, Discover Your Strengths*, you'll be able to see when people are and are not using their strengths in management, and you can begin thinking about how you can best manage others by most effectively using your own strengths.

10. Other opportunities for leadership development within the college experience

In addition to the opportunities listed above, the college experience provides countless opportunities to develop your leadership abilities. For example, most colleges provide opportunities for students to become involved in musical performances, drama, theater, and other artistic modes of expression. Each of these offers rich opportunities to develop leadership strengths.

Becoming a strengths-based leader is a process that begins with who you are, then moves to what you do. Here are principles that you can follow to become a person who leads on the basis of strengths.

- Realize that you do not need to be in a formal leadership role to provide valuable leadership.

- Identify the specific leadership functions in which you have strengths.

- Lead with your strengths as you work in groups to help them reach goals.

- Pay close attention to others in the organization, and try to identify their strengths.

- Encourage others in the organization by helping them to see the positive contributions they are making *as they use their strengths productively*.

- Create opportunities for others to develop and use their strengths — opportunities to do what they do best.

- Become clear about your personal goals, and help the members of the organization focus on the goals they want to accomplish.

This aspect of becoming a strengths-based leader cannot be emphasized enough: Be intentional. Purposely look at each college experience in terms of learning something about how to be a leader. It doesn't matter if you are a leader or a follower. In either role, you can learn something about leadership.

Chapter VIII

APPLYING STRENGTHS FOR
ACADEMIC ACHIEVEMENT

Prior to this point, this book helped you identify, understand, and appreciate your talents. It then showed you how to develop your talents into strengths. Now, it's time to help you learn how to apply your strengths toward greater levels of achievement in the many aspects of academics.

Four key factors capture the basic aspects you should consider when planning an education that will lead to personal excellence.

Four Key Factors That Will Determine Your Achievements in Academics, Career, and Beyond

1. Your beliefs about your strengths to achieve

Never underestimate the power of what you believe — it will directly affect your achievements. What you believe about your strengths can affect *whether you will even attempt to achieve*. Your beliefs directly influence your emotions, attitudes, behavior patterns, and motivation.

2. How well you know, understand, and value your strengths

One of our primary goals is to increase your understanding of and appreciation for the strengths you already have. This forms the basis for increasing your confidence and for building achievement patterns.

3. The extent to which you develop and apply your strengths

You should provide the initiative for designing your education around your strengths. This is likely to result in a superior education. Think about it. You won't be "getting" an education; you will be "creating" one. And the education you will be creating will be based on who you really are and the person you have the capacity to become.

4. Your motivations, desires, and goal-setting practices

Numerous studies identify motivation as the single most important factor in academic achievement and graduation from college. Specifically, they point to two important motivational dynamics: First, you must have multiple motives for achieving and persisting. Second, these motives must be important to you personally. Having only one reason for achieving (for example, to make more money or to please someone else) usually results in lesser achievement.

Strategies for Applying Your Strengths in Academics

To help you determine how you can best apply your strengths to achieve in academics, we have collected feedback from thousands of top-achieving college students. Through interviews, focus groups, case studies, and surveys, we have gathered insights about how these successful students perceived and applied their strengths in several areas of academics.

Now, it's time to take a look at strategies that can help you use strengths in your Signature Themes for achievement in various aspects of your academic life. Once again, locate and examine the strategies that are customized to your Signature Themes. As you do this, you may want to consider the items that are already helping you achieve and those that may help you achieve at an even greater level of excellence.

Applying Your Strengths in Academics

Applying Achiever Strengths in Academics

These insights and action ideas can help you apply Achiever strengths to achieve in various aspects of your academic life.

General Academic Life

☐ Set at least one clearly defined and measurable goal for each of your courses at the beginning of the term. Document your progress toward each objective in an academic achievement journal.

☐ Identify the most important fact, philosophy, concept, or law you learn in each class each week. Notice recurring patterns. Pinpoint discoveries.

☐ Set one or two "stretch" targets, such as earning a specific grade point average, winning honors status, or being named to the dean's list.

☐ Ask to review papers, projects, research studies, or tests of several students who consistently earn higher grades in a class than you do. Emulate — that is, try to equal or surpass — one or two things they do.

☐ Seek opportunities to apply several of the ideas and concepts you have learned. Address groups and conduct demonstrations so others can benefit from what you know.

☐ Ask each of your professors to clarify their expectations for your performance. Emphasize that you intend to exceed the minimum course requirements.

Study Techniques

☐ Review your goals achievement log. Look for evidence that you are progressing toward your objectives. Outline the steps you took to acquire one particular skill or master one key concept.

☐ Pay close attention to your biological clock. Decide when your mind is most alert. Use this insight to your advantage when scheduling time to study.

☐ Decide whether your productivity, efficiency, and ability to retain essential information increases when you study with a tutor, a classmate, a group, or alone.

☐ Observe classmates to discover who shares your commitment to hard work. Form a study group composed of individuals who invest time, effort, and energy in scholarly pursuits.

☐ Reach consensus as a study group about attendance, starting and ending times of meetings, strategies to eliminate distractions, and the sharing of class notes.

☐ List everything you must do to prepare for a test, complete a project, conduct research, or finish an assignment. Prioritize activities. Set a deadline for each one. Then methodically carry out your plan.

Relationships

☐ Intentionally nurture friendships with people who are as driven as you are.

☐ Talk to students taking advanced-level courses in your major field. Ask them to describe the choices they made in the past that contribute to their success today.

☐ Realize that your natural inclination to study for as long as it takes inspires other Achievers. Learn the names of these individuals. Add them to your study buddy network.

☐ Seek opportunities to work with professors on research projects, laboratory experiments, and writing for publications.

Class Selection

☐ Choose challenging but realistic classes taught by instructors who have a reputation for helping students reach their learning goals.

☐ Sequence the order in which you take classes. Each term, enroll in one course that is more demanding than any you have ever taken. Repeat this process each semester.

☐ Recruit diligent, serious, and earnest students to register for the same demanding classes you are taking. Realize that you will challenge one another to excel.

☐ Sign up for classes that cover unfamiliar topics. Understand that you are motivated by challenges.

Extracurricular Activities

☐ Join clubs with members who share your strong work ethic.

☐ Advance toward your academic and career goals by enrolling in rigorous classes, volunteering on campus, performing community service, working part time, and participating in intramural or extramural sports.

☐ Elect to join organizations where your accomplishments will be recognized. Choose groups with goals that align with your own. Insist on establishing deadlines for reaching each objective.

Applying Activator Strengths in Academics

These insights and action ideas can help you apply Activator strengths to achieve in various aspects of your academic life.

General Academic Life

☐ Initiate classroom discussions. Suggest topics. Take sides in debates. Help your fellow students learn more, faster.

☐ Ask questions that you anticipate the instructor to ask on upcoming tests and quizzes.

☐ Instigate conversations with your peers outside the classroom. Center these on topics related to a recent lecture given by your instructor or a visiting professor.

☐ Take charge of small group conversations, projects, presentations, and experiments. Distinguish yourself by transforming plans into tangible results.

☐ Waste no time finishing the first draft of a writing assignment. Immediately seek feedback from a teaching assistant or your professor. Incorporate some of their constructive suggestions in your second draft.

Study Techniques

☐ Lead study groups. Participate in the life of the mind. Urge members to share their best ideas. Give timid individuals permission to explore topics, raise questions, and work on projects.

☐ Jot down one or two key thoughts as you read an article, story, or the directions from a project. Use these insights to shape the group's discussions.

☐ Draw quiet individuals into conversations, debates, planning, and discussions. Call on them by name. Probe when they respond to questions with one or two word answers.

☐ Read ahead to prepare for class lectures. Compose two or three questions, not in the textbook, to ask the instructor. Intentionally change the classroom atmosphere from one of passive listening to active participation.

☐ Stay physically active to remain mentally engaged in your studies. Eat. Pace. Take breaks to stretch. Test your ideas with your study group. Press for their honest opinions.

Relationships

☐ Surround yourself with individuals who are restless to start working on projects and assignments. Associate with people who welcome and respond to your directives.

☐ Identify classmates who automatically know when the time for planning has expired and the time for action has arrived.

☐ Initiate conversations with professors outside the classroom. Make appointments with them to confirm expectations, clarify course requirements, and establish deadlines.

☐ Volunteer to chair group discussions, facilitate brainstorming sessions, or spearhead projects. Observe your classmates' relief at not having to be in charge.

Class Selection

☐ Choose a major field of study about which you are passionate. Realize your success hinges on your being fully engaged. Opt for courses that involve hands-on activities, lively verbal exchanges, and interesting experiments.

☐ Check the course syllabus for information about projects, field trips, extra reading, and independent study options. Avoid classes that restrict your pace and methods. Honor your need for speedy results and changes of pace.

☐ Attack your assignments immediately. Refuse to procrastinate. Turn in your work ahead of schedule. Enjoy the satisfaction of being done. Analyze how you avoid the pitfalls of analysis paralysis and overpreparation.

☐ Persuade your professor to give you permission to invent your own assignments with the understanding that they must satisfy the course requirements and learning objectives.

Extracurricular Activities

☐ Join clubs and try out for athletic teams with jam-packed rosters of events. Avoid groups with a reputation for meeting a lot but accomplishing very little.

☐ Volunteer for activities such as constructing a Habitat for Humanity^{SM} house, serving as a Big Brother^{SM} or Big Sister^{SM}, acting in community theatre productions, conducting nature walks, running to raise funds for worthwhile causes, or coaching a youth team.

☐ Be the change agent for a stalled project. Study the original action plan. Determine why momentum was lost. Convince group members they can put the undertaking back on course. Recruit several energetic individuals to help implement the new initiative.

☐ Campaign for an office in campus government. Influence potential voters to cast their ballots for you.

Applying Adaptability Strengths in Academics

These insights and action ideas can help you apply Adaptability strengths to achieve in various aspects of your academic life.

General Academic Life

☐ Live in the moment. Calm yourself before an exam with positive self-talk. Recall your personal history of dealing with surprises on tests.

☐ Leverage your ability to not feel overwhelmed by multifaceted assignments. Document three to five instances during the day when you successfully juggled competing tasks.

☐ Understand that you can balance academic demands with social commitments, extracurricular activities, and part-time jobs. Describe how you managed to make progress on all fronts last week.

☐ Challenge yourself by taking courses that involve experiments. Compare your flexibility to that of various classmates. Notice how you make adjustments to produce desired outcomes.

Study Techniques

☐ Analyze your study habits. Do you plan and then improvise as circumstances change? Or do you improvise minute by minute rather than plan?

☐ Choose study partners who are serious yet share your easy-going, relaxed work style. Avoid individuals who are tense and anxious. Make a list of potential study buddies.

☐ Look for irony, humor, and the unexpected in your studies. Stimulate your own and others' thinking by discussing the relevance of each discovery.

☐ Make notes about how your study habits vary depending on the situation. Ask yourself these questions: Do I need the pressure of a test or deadline to force me to study? When am I most likely to ignore intriguing distractions? Least likely?

☐ Designate places you can retreat when you need to give your full attention to your studies. Choose venues where the potential for interruptions and extraneous noise is significantly reduced.

Relationships

☐ Surround yourself with individuals who, like you, pause to take in the world's loveliness as it appears. Identify people who automatically put aside what they are doing to watch a sunset, listen to rustling leaves, or enjoy the arts.

☐ Help classmates, coworkers, and friends overcome difficulties that stymie their progress. Capitalize on your ability to take things as they are rather than rail against life's surprises.

☐ Encourage some people to turn to you when plans must be modified or altogether scrapped. List the people who realize you are approachable and responsive.

☐ Invite one or two highly organized and time-conscious people to become your study buddies. Discuss ahead of time how they can help you be more efficient. Explain how you can infuse fun into their studies.

Class Selection

☐ Follow your interests when choosing classes. Keep your options for a major open until you have explored several disciplines. Partner with an advisor who can help you accelerate your decision-making process to avoid additional tuition costs.

☐ Register for more classes than you intend to take. After the first week of class, drop elective courses you find uninteresting.

☐ Transfer out of classes taught by instructors whose teaching style bores you. Transfer into the classes of professors who stimulate students' thinking.

☐ Take advantage of the drop-add period. Note the date by which you must complete this process without risking a failing grade or loss of money.

Extracurricular Activities

☐ Join organizations that sponsor events that demand flexibility in terms of planning as well as execution. Capitalize on your ability to monitor and adjust.

☐ Convince teammates of the importance of not fighting change. Outline the benefits of letting go of the original plan in order to try a new process.

☐ Recall two or three instances where you successfully redirected the emotional energy of people paralyzed by unexpected news or sudden changes in the group's plans.

☐ Consider participating in extemporaneous speech tournaments or improvisational theater. Play to your ability to capitalize on each moment.

Applying Analytical Strengths in Academics

These insights and action ideas can help you apply Analytical strengths to achieve in various aspects of your academic life.

General Academic Life

☐ Examine data, collect facts, and read material for discussions. Anticipate problems. Ask questions to discover others' perspectives on issues. Clarify your own position.

☐ Reduce situations, problems, opportunities, projects, assignments, and debates to their key components. Stay two to three steps ahead of everyone else's thinking by pinpointing cause-and-effect relationships.

☐ Deduce the consequences of someone's decisions, inaction, and pronouncements. Use logic to trace the effects of scientific breakthroughs, ethical lapses, and legal judgments.

☐ Prove to your classmates that there is an equal and opposite reaction to every action.

☐ Read assignments before class. Find information to support or discount the position taken by the author of the textbook.

☐ Reinforce your understanding of the subject matter by reorganizing and expanding your classroom notes. Insert subtopics and subpoints.

Study Techniques

☐ Notice the subtle nuances of a subject. Question the authors' conclusions. Flag topics for scrutiny. Refuse to blindly accept whatever appears on the printed page.

☐ Assess why you do quite well in one course but not as well in others. Evaluate your study habits, note taking, listening, capacity for asking questions, and reading comprehension.

☐ Draw mind maps to illustrate the placement of each element of a theory or aspect of a concept as well as a story plot. Investigate until you logically link facts or numerical data with results.

☐ Record questions as you read. Ask: "What is missing here?" "What questions should the author have answered?" "What biases are evident and not so evident?"

☐ Make sense of discussions. Write what you heard and said. Identify comments, conclusions, and arguments that lack supporting facts or data.

Relationships

☐ Break down situations. How is the same set of facts likely to be interpreted by someone older than you? Younger than you? From a different cultural, ethnic, religious, socio-economic, or racial background?

☐ Identify your biases before taking sides on an issue. Evaluate your own thinking before challenging others' biases.

☐ Incorporate into your study group individuals who thoughtfully assess the value of information, details, research findings, evidence, people's comments, and events.

☐ Refrain from saying what is on your mind until you have figured out everything. Realize that this reduces the tension between yourself and others.

Class Selection

☐ Select professors with reputations for presenting lessons in a logical, sequential manner. Avoid instructors who present a confusing jumble of unrelated ideas, facts, theories, illustrations, or philosophies.

☐ Select courses that will use your talent for critical thinking. Be open to the sciences and mathematics as well as literature, history, and the arts.

☐ Consider the soundness, validity, and reliability of information presented in your textbooks and by your professors.

☐ Dismiss erroneous statements, flawed theories, and illogical conclusions, as well as prejudiced opinions. Risk being the solitary voice of reason.

Extracurricular Activities

☐ Gravitate to organizations known for their commitment to use of logic and reason.

☐ Volunteer to serve on campus committees charged with proposing recommendations to key decision-making bodies such as the student senate, the school board, and the state legislature.

☐ Join the debate team. Delve deeply into the chosen topic. Fully research both sides of the issue. Prepare logical arguments from both perspectives. Continue to build both cases to clearly define strong positions.

☐ Accompany an athletic coach to scouting and practice sessions for a week. Identify three to five ways you can combine your love for a particular sport with your analytical abilities. Consider plays the team could run, or the types of physical talents required for the various positions.

Applying Arranger Strengths in Academics

These insights and action ideas can help you apply Arranger strengths to achieve in various aspects of your academic life.

General Academic Life

☐ Note all assignments, tests, and appointments on a calendar. Use your planner to coordinate your personal and academic activities.

☐ Read all directions prior to taking tests. Allot appropriate time to each section of the examination.

☐ Be prepared to stop working on a current project and begin a new one in case the situation changes.

☐ Keep all notes related to a topic on one page. Make them easily accessible for studying, test taking, and research papers.

Study Techniques

☐ Prioritize what to study. Identify the most important tasks based on deadlines, percentage of final grade, and difficulty. Balance your workload.

☐ Underline, highlight, and take notes in margins of books. Summarize main ideas.

☐ Pick locations where you can study. Figure out why certain environments are better for particular subjects.

☐ Schedule study breaks to clear your mind. Check on other projects, or make phone calls.

☐ Break each study session into distinct modules. Plan time to read, write, work on projects, eat, sleep, exercise, and socialize.

Relationships

☐ Recognize that you can change your personal agenda to meet others' demands. Ponder how you readjust your living and working environment to help others reach their goals.

☐ Assemble people to work on major class projects and prepare for exams. Name the ways you help your study buddies distribute and redistribute learning tasks.

☐ Create opportunities for group members to teach each other.

☐ Plan activities to mark the end of projects and success on exams.

Class Selection

☐ Help your instructor plan class projects. Volunteer to assemble needed supplies. Distribute materials to students and collect them at the end of class.

☐ Figure out ways for your classmates to manage their workloads so that they complete projects on or before the due date.

☐ Suggest independent study options to your advisors and professors. Design your own curriculum.

☐ Examine the course catalogs from other schools in the vicinity. Substitute some of these courses for ones on your degree or certification plan.

Extracurricular Activities

☐ Orchestrate your study time so that extracurricular activities can fit into your schedule.

☐ Get involved and stay busy. Mix non-academic projects, appointments, meetings, and tasks into your day or week.

☐ Coordinate routine activities, special events, trips, parties, and projects for your teammates.

☐ Mix and match the talents, knowledge, skills, and experience of your classmates to launch a project, move toward a goal, or produce desired outcomes.

Applying Belief Strengths in Academics

These insights and action ideas can help you apply Belief strengths to achieve in various aspects of your academic life.

General Academic Life

☐ Write an academic mission statement for yourself. Integrate your core values, such as a leaving the world better than you found it, curing AIDS, ending violence, or affirming the dignity of each human being.

☐ Discover ways to weave your core values into routine classroom assignments. Write and speak about topics directly related to your beliefs.

☐ Read about individuals who stood up for their convictions in the face of resistance. Determine who inspired these people to dedicate their lives to great and noble causes.

☐ Debate the issue: Money is the true source of happiness. Argue for and against this proposition. Ask yourself, "How was my position strengthened when I could incorporate my beliefs into the argument? How was my position weakened when I had to defend the opposing point of view?"

Study Techniques

☐ List your top three to five beliefs on a piece of paper you can use as a bookmark. Filter whatever you are reading and hearing through the lenses of these core values.

☐ Assess whether you are allocating enough time to classes, projects, and assignments that add meaning to your life.

☐ Suggest alternative topics for reading and research to your professors. Match your preferred assignments to one or more of your core values.

☐ Form a study group of individuals with whom you share one or more important belief. Ask each member to describe how these core values contribute to his or her success as a student.

Relationships

☐ Tell your classmates and professors about the ideas, causes, and projects you are most passionate about.

☐ Encourage others to tell you when your intensity inspires them and when it overwhelms them. Maintain an ongoing dialogue to ensure that they understand you.

☐ State what you believe is right and wrong. Help others grasp what you value and why you value it.

☐ Notice instances when you willingly inconvenienced yourself to come to the aid of a specific person or group. Ask, "Which of my core values drove this behavior?"

Class Selection

☐ Enroll in ethics classes. Learn to evaluate the rightness of decisions in fields such as science, medicine, business, government, religion, and environmental protection.

☐ Risk advocating your beliefs in class discussions as well as conversations with classmates and instructors.

☐ Choose courses taught by professors known for their strong beliefs, even when their values clash with yours. Realize that considering the values of others can help you refine your own.

☐ Select classes that challenge you to clarify, reinforce, defend, and live out the guiding principles of your life.

Extracurricular Activities

☐ Figure out ways to spend quality time with your family. Make a point of going home or calling to show you are thinking of them on birthdays and special holidays.

☐ Consider running for a campus office. Build your campaign platform on values-oriented issues that matter greatly to you. Inform potential voters what you stand for and why.

☐ Practice speaking a foreign language by helping a refugee family adapt to their new country and its customs.

☐ Serve meals at a local homeless shelter. Deliver Meals on Wheels. Take time to visit with each shut-in.

Applying Command Strengths in Academics

These insights and action ideas can help you apply Command strengths to achieve in various aspects of your academic life.

General Academic Life

☐ Ask probing and pointed questions during discussions and lectures by professors. Realize that your questioning mind accelerates your learning.

☐ Take charge of your learning. Play the lead role in shaping your degree or certification plan. Refuse to leave these decisions to an advisor.

☐ Challenge facts presented in textbooks, the media, and class presentations. Critique your instructors and classmates. Search for the truth.

☐ When a particularly interesting class discussion is ended due to time constraints, express to your professor your wish that he or she continue the discussion in an office visit.

Study Techniques

☐ Join study groups known for debating ideas, theories, and problems.

☐ Use your Command to clarify rather than intimidate. Understand that some clear-thinking individuals may become flustered under pressure.

☐ Give frank feedback to instructors on what you like and dislike about their class in general, and about their assignments in particular.

☐ Develop hypotheses and thesis statements that you must defend in writing or oral presentations. Recognize that you are more engaged when you must build a case to support your ideas.

☐ Play devil's advocate — that is, argue the opposing view — for fun. Warn people that you like to draw them into debates.

Relationships

☐ Assume the leadership role in groups, especially when you have knowledge, skills, expertise, and experience others lack.

☐ Notice which classmates rely on you to ask the professor questions. Provide this service for those who are intimidated by the instructor's knowledge or demeanor.

☐ Study your mannerisms, vocal tone, and content of your messages when talking with authority figures. Pinpoint how you present yourself as a person worthy of their time and undivided attention.

☐ Explore ways that you can serve others by giving orders and making demands. Identify individuals who are comfortable and content following your lead.

Class Selection

☐ Select classes that require you to plan your own curriculum. Acknowledge your desire to make your own academic decisions.

☐ Take classes in which you are expected to voice your opinions, argue, draw conclusions, take sides, and make recommendations.

☐ Choose classes taught by instructors who take a position and demand that students challenge it.

☐ Enroll in courses with professors who are secure enough to welcome your combative learning style.

Extracurricular Activities

☐ Gravitate to organizations in which you can envision yourself being a key decision maker.

☐ Realize that you threaten some people with your forceful style.

☐ Opt to participate in activities where you must persuade people to embrace your ideas, plans, solutions, or philosophies.

☐ Join groups where you are expected to sell things, solicit donations, and raise money.

Applying Communication Strengths in Academics

These insights and action ideas can help you apply Communication strengths to achieve in various aspects of your academic life.

General Academic Life

☐ Participate in class discussions. Enhance your own and others' comprehension by talking through the key points.

☐ Respond to questions with thought-provoking answers.

☐ Illustrate scholarly concepts with real-life examples. Help others learn in the process.

☐ Capture your audience's interest by telling stories to amplify an idea, concept, theory, scientific law, philosophical point, ethical quandary, or historic event.

Study Techniques

☐ Converse about the subject matter until you fully understand it.

☐ Tell others about your solutions, theories, concepts, and ideas before presenting them in class. Acknowledge that this is how you refine your thinking.

☐ Notice how your classmates rely on you to engage the professor in dialogue. Realize that you are quite comfortable doing this.

☐ Entertain your study group with anecdotes that make history, mathematics, science, languages, or the arts come alive in their minds.

Relationships

☐ Take the pressure off quiet, timid individuals by doing most of the talking.

☐ Cheer up people with accounts of your own and others' humorous escapades.

☐ Plan at least four meetings each term with professors who are good listeners. Take advantage of the fact that they expect you to do most of the talking.

☐ Express your philosophical views, goals, pet peeves, and opinions so others can learn about you as a person.

Class Selection

☐ Take classes from professors who encourage students to interrupt lectures to share stories or offer examples that amplify a concept.

☐ Select classes in which you will be graded for participation in class discussions.

☐ Register for courses that require you to make presentations.

☐ Enroll in theatre arts, speech, and communications classes.

Extracurricular Activities

☐ Affiliate with a speakers' bureau in which the members address campus and community groups.

☐ Try out for the speech team. Concentrate on dramatic interpretation to hone your storytelling skills.

☐ Audition for plays even if you are not a theatre major.

☐ Campaign for elected office, or be a candidate's spokesperson.

Applying Competition Strengths in Academics

These insights and action ideas can help you apply Competition strengths to achieve in various aspects of your academic life.

General Academic Life

☐ Regard grades as your scorecard. Invest more effort in classes where the results of tests, papers, and projects are posted for all to see.

☐ Monitor your grade point average by the week, month, or academic term. Compare your class ranking to that of your closest rivals. Realize that earning the highest GPA pressures you to excel.

☐ Clarify how professors weight class participation, final exams, presentations, laboratory experiments, and research projects. Continuously monitor your grades and class standing.

☐ Study your opponents, that is, your classmates. Identify each one's strengths. Evaluate their study strategies. Continually compare your results to theirs.

Study Techniques

☐ Seek out highly competitive people and study with them. Know that you will push each other to learn more, faster. Figure out how to manage the inevitable undercurrent of tension that will exist.

☐ Pit yourself against a fellow student to increase your chances of being the first person to finish the paper, test, or project.

☐ Establish measurable and meaningful academic goals. Use these to force yourself to reach the highest levels of productivity, mastery, or quality.

☐ Find out who is the best in your classes or major area of study. Investigate what they routinely do to be number one.

☐ Quiz your professors until they outline their criteria for earning the highest grades in their classes. Explain that you aim to understand the material better than anyone else in the class.

Relationships

☐ Intentionally surround yourself with competitive people.

☐ Aim to know something special about every person in the class by the end of the first month. Use these insights to your advantage when you vie against them.

☐ Help classmates understand that you are hardwired to have the last word in casual conversation, classroom discussion, or formal debate.

Class Selection

☐ Apply at universities and departments within universities where admission is highly competitive. Make sure that objective, meaningful, and measurable criteria are used to determine who is selected.

☐ Take advanced-level classes to enhance the odds of winning important academic scholarships, grants, internships, and fellowships.

☐ Opt for classes in which you receive rewards for your grades.

☐ Select instructors who encourage rivalry between students.

Extracurricular Activities

☐ Try out for the debate or speech team. Audition for a play, first chair in a section of the orchestra, or a featured dancing role.

☐ Play competitive sports. Risk being a walk-on to win a spot on an athletic team.

☐ Check your department's bulletin boards for opportunities to enter contests. Gravitate to contests sponsored by student and professional organizations in your major area of study.

☐ Run for leadership positions such as student senate, class president, club officer, or sorority/fraternity chairs. Campaign to win.

Applying Connectedness Strengths in Academics

These insights and action ideas can help you apply Connectedness strengths to achieve in various aspects of your academic life.

General Academic Life

☐ Ask yourself, "What life lessons am I supposed to learn today through my studies and the challenges they present? What is at work here that is much more important than passing a test or getting a good grade?"

☐ Search for linkages between your coursework and what you are being called to contribute to the entire human family today and in the future.

☐ Examine how your life is inextricably tied to people in other parts of the world and from the past. Name as many of these connections as you possibly can.

☐ Find ways to build bridges of understanding between classmates as well as between students and their professors. Realize that you are motivated to show people how world events and close-to-home circumstances bind each individual to all humankind.

☐ Start each day by reading an inspirational verse or a piece of scripture from your faith. Sit in silence with these words for 10-15 minutes. Open yourself up to surprising discoveries about how to approach your studies and people.

☐ Keep a journal. Let your ideas and feelings flow freely. Write without editing. Find purpose and meaning in your personal and academic life.

Study Techniques

☐ Pray for guidance before you begin studying. Ask that your mind be freed of worries and distractions. Implore that you can truly trust that all will be well.

☐ Concentrate on your breathing before starting a test, making a presentation, or working on a project. Unite yourself with students around the world who are facing similar challenges at this very moment.

☐ Silence competing scholarly demands of your life by practicing daily meditation. Master the art of letting go. Embrace the art of living in the present moment.

☐ Be mindful of the abundance of good things. Realize that more than one student can earn a good grade or receive the professor's approval.

☐ Energize your body, heighten your awareness, and soothe your soul with inspiring background music. Create a calm environment in which to study, work on projects, solve problems, research, write, and prepare for exams.

Relationships

☐ Converse with individuals who realize that life is a complex web of interdependence among all human beings, living things, events, and inanimate objects.

☐ Share with curious observers how and why you can remain calm in the midst of uncertainty, losses, successes, defeats, progress, and setbacks.

☐ Help others understand that you view all life as a continuous, ever-widening circle without beginning or end. Explain how every thought, word, and deed impacts people far and near.

☐ Bring ideas, projects, and relationships full circle. Tie together loose ends. Describe how your experiences and studies benefit individuals and all humankind.

Class Selection

☐ Enroll in comparative religion studies. Better understand today's news events by comparing and contrasting the beliefs of the world's great religions.

☐ Find colleges in your area offering courses in the study of dreams. Look for listings in the departments of psychology, religious studies, and theology.

☐ Select history classes in which you can research events through the lens of conflicting religious doctrines and principles held as truth by some groups.

☐ Register for theology, philosophy, and ethics classes to broaden your thinking. Integrate what you learn into your other coursework.

Extracurricular Activities

☐ Consider meeting with a spiritual director every four to six weeks. Describe instances of being keenly aware of the "invisible hand" of a life force, higher power, or God acting in your life. Be attentive to patterns and recurring questions.

☐ Get involved in campus groups and ministries to nurture your faith tradition or introduce you to new forms of spirituality.

☐ Opt for nontraditional school vacations. Volunteer to build a Habitat for Humanity^SM house, travel to a third-world nation to help in a medical clinic, clean up an inner-city neighborhood, or work with urban families to plant a neighborhood vegetable garden.

☐ Mentor at-risk students during the school year. Become a reading tutor for adults. Teach English to immigrant and refugee families. Record books for the blind. Serve as a camp counselor for handicapped or terminally ill children.

Applying Consistency Strengths in Academics

These insights and action ideas can help you apply Consistency strengths to achieve in various aspects of your academic life.

General Academic Life

☐ Insist that your professors set the same clear expectations for everyone in the class. Make sure that you know exactly what is required to earn the grades you desire.

☐ Understand precisely how class participation, research, laboratory work, presentations, and examinations will be factored into your final grade for the course.

☐ Inform others that routines are important to your success. Explain how they lend an air of familiarity to all the coursework in your major area of study.

☐ Finalize your entire degree or certification plan as early in your collegiate career as possible. Each term, double-check your plan to ensure you are in compliance with graduation requirements.

☐ Express your belief that everyone deserves the same opportunities to earn good grades on tests, projects, research papers, or experiments. Help professors and classmates understand why you become upset when someone is given special treatment.

Study Techniques

☐ Anticipate what you need to do to earn the grade you want in each class. Set up and adhere to a study routine. Realize that you excel when your life has a rhythm to it.

☐ Make a habit of studying at the same time each day. Designate a specific study area and equip it appropriately. Replenish supplies on a specific day of the week.

☐ Establish predictable and uniform patterns for doing different kinds of assignments, such as writing, researching, calculating, and rehearsing speeches.

☐ Heighten your awareness of how much time you require to complete each assignment. Honor the ways you study best rather than mimicking those of successful classmates.

☐ Balance all the facts when conducting research, making a presentation, or writing a report. Seek to remove biases by being objective.

☐ Create study rituals that suit your thinking and learning style. Read ahead. Write down questions to which you want answers. Highlight key ideas, steps, and concepts. Take notes on note cards, in a spiral notebook, or in computer files.

Relationships

☐ Understand that your predictability makes you a valuable study buddy. Partner with classmates whose need for routines and processes mirrors your own.

☐ Inform people about your need for uniformity. Help them understand how they can benefit from consistency.

☐ Recruit some classmates and professors with enough patience to help you recognize the need to make changes in procedures, study patterns, and routines.

Class Selection

☐ Identify similarities and differences in your professors' teaching styles. Choose classes taught by instructors whose approach matches your learning style.

☐ Avoid taking courses from professors who play favorites, change assignment requirements unexpectedly, and fail to abide by the rules they set at the start of the term.

☐ Make a list of courses of study that naturally incorporate routines, processes, and procedures. Consider specific science, mathematics, accounting, music, engineering, and law programs.

Extracurricular Activities

☐ Join clubs and teams known for their adherence to practice and rehearsal schedules.

☐ Help with special events that have a long history of doing things the same way from one year to the next.

☐ Assume accountability for monitoring compliance to rules for membership drives, fundraising, and contests.

☐ Volunteer to maintain the records of an organization. Ensure that accepted procedures are followed in meetings, and reports are properly submitted.

Applying Context Strengths in Academics

These insights and action ideas can help you apply Context strengths to achieve in various aspects of your academic life.

General Academic Life

☐ Associate with individuals and groups that specialize in the study of specific events, personalities, and periods in history.

☐ Create a historical frame of reference for whatever you study. Research political, natural, military, and religious events of that period. Delve into the lives of contemporary leaders, scientists, artists, explorers, and philosophers.

☐ Critique required reading for classes by locating other credible sources of information. Refuse to let your thinking be limited to the professor's syllabus.

☐ Understand that you are attracted to institutions of learning with a rich history and a long tradition.

☐ Seek opportunities to study with reputable, recognized, and knowledgeable historians who also are master teachers.

☐ Attend lecture series in which leading figures of your time speak about their experiences in global leadership, diplomacy, military affairs, business, science, or the arts. Prepare a question to pose during the Q&A session or book signing.

Study Techniques

☐ Hypothesize your own theories for specific historic events. Rely on public records, surveys, correspondence, and legislation to develop a study brief.

☐ Consider your own history of test taking. Identify your best performances. Spot patterns. Prepare for today's examinations by replicating study techniques that have worked for you in the past.

☐ Overcome obstacles placed in your path by a professor by conferring with former students of this individual. Ask questions to learn from the experiences of individuals who excelled.

☐ Complement your reading and research assignments with additional sources of information, such as recorded speeches, transcripts of court proceedings, or vintage interviews with key figures and their contemporaries.

☐ Tape record interviews with individuals who lived through significant periods of history, such as the Great Depression, wars, terrorist attacks, political scandals, and boom times.

☐ Find photographs, paintings, drawings, blueprints, news film, videos, costumes, recipes, historical reproductions, almanacs, and costumes to bring a historic epoch to life.

Relationships

☐ Help people understand that you need to know about their past experiences — personal and academic — so you can feel comfortable working with them on projects and in study groups.

☐ Decipher your methods for building a historical basis for your relationships with specific family members, friends, teammates, classmates, instructors, and coworkers.

☐ Ask professors about themselves on the first day of class. Inquire into their influences as children and their academic backgrounds. Read their master's theses, doctoral dissertations, books, articles, lectures, and speeches.

☐ Attend class reunions. Reminisce about your school days with former classmates, faculty, and administrators. Pose questions to discover what individuals have done with their lives since graduation.

Class Selection

☐ Choose classes taught by professors who examine cause-and-effect relationships between the actions of historic figures and the consequences they produce. Avoid history courses that require nothing beyond rote memorization of facts, names, and dates.

☐ Enroll in classes that allow students to study original documents and artifacts. Review the syllabus for information about field trips to museums, battlefields, archives, and theatrical productions based on historic events.

☐ Register for courses such as comparative religion, geography, economics, science, philosophy, and the arts to better understand the root causes of today's wars, alliances, financial policies, treaties, and trade agreements.

☐ Opt for classes in which you can write papers, make presentations, re-create past events, or impersonate historic figures to fulfill course requirements.

Extracurricular Activities

☐ Join a genealogy society or club. Trace your own or someone else's family tree.

☐ Serve as the historian of your fraternity, sorority, honor society, or campus organizations.

☐ Collect and archive memorabilia from events throughout the years. Volunteer to work with the campus historian to gain hands-on experience.

☐ Form a book club whose members read and then discuss autobiographies, biographies, history books, or even historic fiction.

Applying Deliberative Strengths in Academics

These insights and action ideas can help you apply Deliberative strengths to achieve in various aspects of your academic life.

General Academic Life

☐ Attend all lectures and class sessions — make sure you don't miss anything. Be thorough in your preparation for a class by reading ahead and reviewing class notes to avoid being caught off guard.

☐ Before visiting a professor during office hours, prepare thoroughly by making a list of items and questions you wish to discuss.

☐ Schedule regular appointments with your counselors to be well aware of your options and to make sure you are on track.

☐ When you receive a class syllabus, highlight the due dates of readings, assignments, papers, and tests. You may feel more comfortable knowing everything that will be required of you.

☐ Always be well prepared for class. You will feel more comfortable and confident talking in class when you are sure of the validity of what you have to say and the completeness of your thoughts.

☐ When taking a test, go through the questions slowly, concentrating on the ones you are more sure of first. Address the others later so that you have time to complete the exam.

Study Techniques

☐ When reading assignments, be sure to allow yourself plenty of time to finish; know your own pace. Take notes on what you read, and study your notes for exams.

☐ Work extra problems just to be sure you understand the material.

☐ If you work best alone, study on your own before engaging in group discussions. This will allow you to reinforce what you have learned with the group, without needing to rely on the group.

☐ Form questions as you study, and make sure you have answers to them before taking an exam.

Relationships

☐ Choose friends who have academic goals similar to yours, so you reinforce one another in your serious pursuit of studying.

☐ Make frequent visits during office hours to develop relationships with one or two professors or teaching assistants whose advice you feel you can trust.

☐ When forming study groups, be selective about whom you study with. Choose responsible, serious people like yourself who will be well prepared and focus on the task at hand.

Class Selection

☐ Before choosing a class, look at the class syllabus, check the number of books, and learn more about the professor. Don't be caught off guard on the first day of class.

☐ Double check with your advisor to ensure that a class meets the requirements that you need.

☐ You are most comfortable in classes where you are well aware of expectations, where the discussions are serious, and where the time is used well. Before you enroll in a class, get the opinion of peers with similar interests to yours who have already taken the class.

Extracurricular Activities

☐ Look carefully at the many organizations or clubs that you might join to pinpoint those that pique your interest. Attend a couple of meetings to narrow down to one or two that seem to fit you best.

☐ Rely on your own judgment to know the types of activities that will be most enjoyable to you. Purely social activities without further purpose will most likely feel like a waste of time to you.

☐ Look for job opportunities and internships in which you will be recognized for your seriousness and your ability to raise questions about decisions that are made.

Applying Developer Strengths in Academics

These insights and action ideas can help you apply Developer strengths to achieve in various aspects of your academic life.

General Academic Life

☐ During lectures, take down facts that are new, enlightening, interesting, or humorous. Share your observations with others from the class.

☐ Reflect back to what you have learned from a certain professor and how that has impacted you in your life.

☐ Motivate yourself by tutoring or helping someone else in the class to understand concepts you have gained from the lecture, the reading, and the discussion.

☐ Keep an ongoing list of your key learning experiences. Track your own progress and growth.

Study Techniques

☐ Explain to a friend, fellow student, teaching assistant, or professor what you have learned from a book, lecture, or other source.

☐ Form study groups in which you can teach as well as learn from others.

☐ Identify a few classmates on whom you can rely to be your study partners.

☐ Pretend that you are going to explain to others what you are trying to learn. This will help you retain more information and improve your comprehension.

☐ Try studying by yourself first, to understand the information, then help others if they need help. One of the best ways to reinforce your learning is to teach others.

Relationships

☐ Always have one or more mentors, and let them know what they add to your life. Consult them regularly.

☐ Help your friends choose developmental experiences.

☐ Coach friends who have a specific goal or focus in mind (such as running a marathon or losing weight). Encourage them in their progress.

Class Selection

☐ Enroll in classes with group projects, specifically those that include community service opportunities.

☐ Enroll in classes with tutoring and discussion groups in which you can learn from others as well as help others learn by discussing and explaining concepts to one another.

☐ Choose a major that highlights your ability to develop the talents of others (i.e., education or psychology).

☐ Choose classes with a field-studies component that involves working with people. This will provide an opportunity to see tangible growth experiences of others and observe how what you learn can be used.

Extracurricular Activities

☐ Become a tutor or a mentor. Find a role in which you can strengthen your own academic skills and help others improve.

☐ Start a club or community service project in which you can impact the achievements of others.

☐ Use your ability and passion to help others by joining organizations that will allow you to exercise your skills in helping others succeed. This will allow you to feel good about what you do and learn from your experiences (for example, become a mentor or peer counselor, join community service organizations).

☐ Consider becoming a counselor in a dorm, where you can provide an environment in which you support the growth of other students.

Applying Discipline Strengths in Academics

These insights and action ideas can help you apply Discipline strengths to achieve in various aspects of your academic life.

General Academic Life

☐ Schedule all assignments, exams, and papers due for the term.

☐ Clean and organize your living space before any major assignments are due or before an examination period.

☐ If you are in a self-paced class or a class with minimal structure, develop your own structure to ensure that you meet the class requirements.

☐ Don't be afraid to color code tasks on your calendar and your textbooks or notes. This will help you focus and prioritize what you are learning and doing.

Study Techniques

☐ Before starting papers, talk to instructors to find out what they expect and how they will grade the papers.

☐ When you come across an unfamiliar word, finish the sentence, look the word up, then reread the sentence.

☐ When preparing for a test, get organized. Collect all notes, have terms defined and facts highlighted and/or listed, and have possible questions available.

☐ When working on a paper, it may be best to make an outline, breaking the topic down into parts that you can work on individually.

☐ Use your discipline to stay ahead in reading assignments. Go over your lecture notes within 12 hours of taking them.

☐ Make a list of all academic tasks that you need to complete for the day. Check items off as you complete them.

Relationships

☐ Find some friends who are as organized as you are. You will not disappoint each other.

☐ Be the organizer for your friends, giving them friendly calls to remind them of when and where you are meeting for dinner, a movie, or other get-togethers.

☐ Delight in a partnership of planning a trip or fun event with a friend. Write down each detail so that the event will meet expectations for both of you.

Class Selection

☐ When choosing classes, arrange them in a way that allows studying during the times that you are more productive. Be realistic.

☐ Take classes that you must fulfill for graduation requirements or your major first.

☐ Choose professors who structure their courses and have clear expectations.

Extracurricular Activities

☐ Volunteer to be a timekeeper for an event. Your accuracy will be appreciated.

☐ Join a group in which you can use your organizational strengths to help plan some major events/goals, breaking down tasks to ensure that deadlines will be met.

☐ Organize a monthly or quarterly "clean up" on your living floor, where people clear away excess papers, files, clothing, etc. Play some music, and arrange to have food brought in to make the task more appealing and fun for others.

Applying Empathy Strengths in Academics

These insights and action ideas can help you apply Empathy strengths to achieve in various aspects of your academic life.

General Academic Life

☐ Seek personal experiences/writings that help you identify with the emotions of the author/researcher/time period you are studying.

☐ Whenever possible, write papers about people. This will strengthen your work as you can pinpoint their points of view.

☐ Keep a journal in which you reflect on what you learned from other people and their passions, fears, joys, and other emotions.

☐ You will sense when friends are academically frustrated in courses you are taking. Let them know that you realize what they are feeling, and continue to encourage and support them.

Study Techniques

☐ As soon as you have an idea, start writing it down, including your feelings. This is a good way to get your ideas onto paper.

☐ When you read, relate as many parts of the reading material (e.g., the characters, the setting, the emotions) as you can to what you have experienced or to people you know. This will make the reading more alive and help you to remember it better.

☐ Ask yourself what the professor wants you to understand about the material, then try to master those topics.

☐ When you are in a study group, be aware of the emotions of people in the group. Help bring those feeling into the open so that others in the group can be aware of the feelings of others and you can keep your focus on the task ahead of you.

Relationships

☐ Discuss issues that are on your mind with your friends. You are usually there for them. Allow them, likewise, to be there for you. Share you feelings with them, because they may not be able to identify feelings as easily as you do.

☐ Use your empathy/listening when conflicts arise at work and in groups.

☐ Be careful not to let those you support overwhelm you. You know that you always try to be there for your friends and family whenever they need you, but it is important to be able to keep your academic goals as a priority.

Class Selection

☐ Think about a major such as education or psychology, which could allow you to use your empathy in your future career.

☐ Choose professors who are known for their Empathy talents as well as for their academic expertise.

☐ Classes that involve reading novels will provide you with an avenue to immerse yourself in the emotions of the characters and to learn from their approaches to situations.

Extracurricular Activities

☐ Become involved in activities, clubs, or organizations that will help you feel like you're making a difference with individuals through your listening/empathy.

☐ If you are interested in helping children, you can help them to better understand their own feelings and help them to sort through their emotions.

☐ Choose one or two people for whom you are a confidante. Many students feel overwhelmed at school; you will understand and help them get through the difficulties that are facing them.

☐ Because you are nonjudgmental and understand the feelings of individuals, you will be a welcome addition to most groups.

Applying Focus Strengths in Academics

These insights and action ideas can help you apply Focus strengths to achieve in various aspects of your academic life.

General Academic Life

☐ Use your focus to link class-related assignments to the knowledge, abilities, and self-management skills you will need to be successful in your future career.

☐ Use your focus to help groups stay on track in classroom discussions or meetings.

☐ If you think that an assignment has no practical value to you, develop one that fits you better, considering your goals, and request permission from your professor to change it.

☐ Evaluate how the material being presented in class relates to your educational and career goals.

☐ When working with others in a small group, help them see how the pieces of a project fit together to accomplish the desired objective.

Study Techniques

☐ Before studying, list everything you will attempt to learn during that time period.

☐ Before writing a paper, outline the main points you plan to address.

☐ Although you can concentrate for long periods of time, regulate yourself to avoid working to exhaustion.

☐ Focus on one issue at a time before moving on to the next issue.

Relationships

☐ Talk to two or three experienced people you admire. Determine the skills, knowledge, and attributes they possess. Ask them how they developed these qualities through their careers.

☐ Identify one or two people in your immediate environment whom you respect. Find out how they became successful.

☐ Choose to associate with focused people.

☐ Identify an alumnus who is in a career that interests you, and spend time with that person to determine how he or she benefited from his or her college experience.

Class Selection

☐ Select classes that will help you fulfill your long-term goals.

☐ Select classes that have defined direction and objectives.

☐ Choose courses where the professor stays on track.

Extracurricular Activities

☐ Look for an internship in an area related to your career goals.

☐ Select activities related to your career goals.

☐ To build on your Focus and not "spread yourself too thin," be selective in the range of activities you are involved in.

Applying Futuristic Strengths in Academics

These insights and action ideas can help you apply Futuristic strengths to achieve in various aspects of your academic life.

General Academic Life

☐ Take risks to learn new insights, even if they are out of your comfort zone. Set academic goals to project you into the future.

☐ Challenge professors with your "What if?" thinking. Encourage them to project beyond to what "might be" in 10, 15, or 20 years.

☐ Know what is expected in each of your classes so you will be able to plan your college years. Visit your academic counselor regularly to keep stretching your thoughts.

☐ Associate with others who enjoy philosophizing about the future.

Study Techniques

☐ Try to really understand what you're studying; don't just memorize. Always relate what you're studying to where you see yourself in the future.

☐ Put some pictures on your wall of what you will be doing and where you see yourself in the future. Look at them often and connect what you are learning to where you want to be.

☐ Take exams seriously and prepare thoroughly. Treat exams as steps toward your future.

☐ Join a group where you take what you are learning and project it into the future. Challenge one another to new visions of the future.

Relationships

☐ Talk about your future goals and dreams with your friends, family, and professors. This will not only keep your goals and dreams top of mind for you, it will also help keep you focused.

☐ Surround yourself with people who will be instrumental in attaining your aspirations. Form strong relationships that can last a long time.

☐ Encourage younger people to be interested in what you enjoy. This helps to reinforce your own goals and dreams, and it also helps them to dream.

☐ Don't let other people's negative comments about your dreams dissuade you from reaching toward them.

Class Selection

☐ Choose classes that will apply to your future career goals.

☐ Pinpoint professors who are futuristic in their thinking, not ones who merely maintain the status quo.

☐ Risk taking a class that will push you to the edge in your thinking.

Extracurricular Activities

☐ Participate in a committee with a forward-thinking leader who can stretch you beyond day-to-day events.

☐ Look for internships that will challenge your thinking and help you reach beyond your current level.

☐ Keep others in your committee or group focused on what can be, frequently sharing the vision that you see.

☐ Join a group that believes that it can impact the future

Applying Harmony Strengths in Academics

These insights and action ideas can help you apply Harmony strengths to achieve in various aspects of your academic life.

General Academic Life

☐ Seek out opinions/ideas from experts. This will help you formulate your own beliefs/philosophy.

☐ You perform best in an environment where people listen to one another and seek to understand each other, rather than one where they try to force their ideas on one another.

☐ You add a calmness or agreeableness to any group.

☐ If the professor frequently changes assignments and due dates in the middle of the term, seek reasons for the changes and share them with classmates, rather than joining the dissension of others.

Study Techniques

☐ Bounce ideas off others whose thinking you respect. They may be able to help you clarify your own ideas.

☐ Read with an open mind. Give the author a chance to explain him/herself. Find the person's ideas that agree with your own and expand from there.

☐ When you are reading something controversial, try to find something you can agree with. Begin your study and analysis there.

☐ When studying in a group, help others see where their viewpoints are congruent.

Relationships

☐ Pick out an expert in each important area of your life and consult with them every eight to ten weeks.

☐ Fill a mediator role with your friends.

☐ Choose friends who listen well to one another and who are at ease with one another.

Class Selection

☐ You will achieve, learn a lot, and enjoy classes in which you learn practical skills and obtain practical knowledge.

☐ Choose classes where there will be a minimum of extreme controversy.

☐ Avoid confrontational, aggressive professors. They may make you so uncomfortable that it may be difficult for you to learn.

Extracurricular Activities

☐ Find a multicultural group, and seek the commonalities in the group. You might enjoy helping them all get to know and appreciate one another.

☐ Volunteer at a senior citizens' home, and help them enjoy some activities together.

☐ Find a group of friends who truly have fun together, who have a lot in common with one another, and who work to make one another happy and support one another. They could become your friends.

Applying Ideation Strengths in Academics

These insights and action ideas can help you apply Ideation strengths to achieve in various aspects of your academic life.

General Academic Life

☐ Take on leadership positions in projects where you can share several ideas and use your creativity.

☐ Take on an independent research project in which you can generate and explore numerous ideas.

☐ Work with a professor in developing a research project, and contribute your creative abilities. You have many ideas to contribute.

☐ Your mind may wander. You can use this to your advantage by letting your thoughts flow freely in class, as long as you think about the subject you are studying.

Study Techniques

☐ As you read an idea, use it as a stimulus for your own further thought and creativity.

☐ As you study, think of different concepts, and invent new ways to present the materials in writing or in graphics. This will invigorate your mind as well as the minds of others.

☐ Allow yourself ample time for thinking. If you rush through a reading assignment, you are less likely to be engaged with it.

☐ Brainstorm with friends about topics you are studying. Let your mind "go wild," knowing that you can sort through the ideas later.

Relationships

☐ Surround yourself with friends who are responsive to listening as well as probing you about your ideas.

☐ Choose a mentor who has the courage to support you in your ideas and who will also challenge you to explore them even further.

☐ You love to generate ideas. Find a partner who would enjoy helping implement your ideas.

Class Selection

☐ Choose classes that involve creative projects rather than simple exams and term papers.

☐ Some classes might not seem to encourage creative expression because of their subject matter. Recognize that you can use your Ideation strengths to create new and stimulating ways to learn.

☐ Select classes taught by professors who enjoy diversity of ideas.

Extracurricular Activities

☐ Join a group that stimulates your ideas and where you feel your ideas are valued.

☐ Involve yourself in a project that allows you to use your creative strengths (i.e., general writing, news magazines, newspapers, journals, graphics, or painting).

☐ Help revive a struggling group. You will have several ideas to restore life into the group. Or, start up a totally new group, generating several ideas about projects in which you might be engaged.

Applying Includer Strengths in Academics

These insights and action ideas can help you apply Includer strengths to achieve in various aspects of your academic life.

General Academic Life

☐ In small groups in class, try to get each student to participate. Ask him or her for opinions.

☐ Ask shy people to walk to class with you.

☐ Research people of different cultures in your community. Invite some people from these cultures to attend a community or university event with you.

☐ Attend lectures or speeches by guest speakers of different nationalities. Introduce yourself to others attending the session, drawing them into a conversation with you.

Study Techniques

☐ Study with other people. If someone is not talking in the group, try to bring him or her into the conversation.

☐ Invite someone who is shy but intelligent to study with you.

☐ Start a small study group of people who seem more hesitant to talk, and include a couple of more verbal people as well.

☐ Search out books on the culture of a prominent ethnic group in your community. Use your new information to help include some people of this culture in activities in which you participate.

Relationships

☐ Expand your relationships to have a diverse group of friends with whom you participate in activities.

☐ You can adjust to many types of people and help them feel welcome. Invite others to your social activities.

☐ Welcome new students to your dorm or living space. Many people assume that others will just make themselves at home. You help them feel a part of the group.

Class Selection

☐ Sign up for classes where you will learn more about the uniqueness of a group of people. Use this information to help them feel included.

☐ Select classes where the professor tries to involve each student.

☐ Select classes that promote diversity.

Extracurricular Activities

☐ Your ability to help others feel like part of the group will make you a valuable member of student organizations and service groups.

☐ Help tutor those who do not have the social or economic privileges you have. Develop or participate in programs that promote diversity.

☐ Volunteer to help with a group such as Special Olympics.

Applying Individualization Strengths in Academics

These insights and action ideas can help you apply Individualization strengths to achieve in various aspects of your academic life.

General Academic Life

☐ Build on your curiosity about people by observing the different ways that people learn and process information.

☐ Read, read, read about people. Their uniqueness fascinates you.

☐ Constantly observe those around you, seeing how you are similar, yet different, from them.

☐ Study some different cultures; the uniqueness will intrigue you.

Study Techniques

☐ Establish a study group with people who possess different talents and perspectives, thereby expanding your own horizons/viewpoints.

☐ As you read a novel, take notes about how the author vividly sets up the uniqueness of each character.

☐ Note how your style of learning, studying, writing papers, and taking tests compares to others. It will help you pinpoint how you are different from others.

☐ As you read about people, make a chart listing specific differences among them. This will hone your observation strengths.

Relationships

☐ See the strengths in people, and encourage them to follow their own dreams. Help them understand and maximize their strengths.

☐ Help your friends/classmates see and appreciate the differences/uniqueness in one another.

☐ Create small support systems, using your Individualization to determine who might benefit from another's insights.

Class Selection

☐ Enroll in classes about people (i.e., literature, sociology, or psychology classes).

☐ Choose classes that promote discussion, bringing out varying beliefs from students.

☐ Choose professors who allow students to make choices regarding their own learning.

Extracurricular Activities

☐ Be a mentor. You will pinpoint a person's individualization and encourage him or her to follow his or her own path.

☐ Involve yourself with activities or organizations that make use of your ability to know each person as an individual (i.e., peer counseling).

☐ Keep a journal with specific observations about individual people. Write some feature articles about people on campus for the school newspaper.

Applying Input Strengths in Academics

These insights and action ideas can help you apply Input strengths to achieve in various aspects of your academic life.

General Academic Life

☐ Save all notes and books from previous classes and create a personal library.

☐ Schedule time for seeking information that goes beyond what is required. The library and the Internet will be valuable in your search.

☐ You enjoy gathering information. You can gain enjoyment from reading a dictionary or encyclopedia, and that is okay.

☐ Start a filing system for interesting articles that you have read.

Study Techniques

☐ Give yourself timelines for completing research papers. Without them, you could continue to read and read, never feeling like you have enough information.

☐ To stay on track while doing required work, put sticky notes on areas you wish to go back and look at.

☐ List extra resources as you study so that you can go back and study them when you have more time.

☐ Prioritize the most critical information to study. Otherwise, you might become distracted by other information that fascinates you but is not as relevant.

Relationships

☐ Share your information with friends. Determine who would be interested in each bit of information, rather than giving all information to everyone.

☐ Seek out professors who would be interested in knowing what you are learning and who will find it stimulating to hear about the questions you are generating through your investigations.

☐ Be aware that the more you know, the more likely it is that others will seek you out for information and see you as highly credible.

Class Selection

☐ Select classes taught by professors who are well read and who keep up to date on the latest research in their field.

☐ Select classes that help you increase your general knowledge base. That would include classes in which research is valued.

☐ Select classes in which class discussion is valued and in which you can share your ideas and the information that you have gleaned.

Extracurricular Activities

☐ Join groups in which you can use your knowledge (e.g., community discussion groups, book clubs, or pre-law society mock trials).

☐ Become involved in extracurricular activities that further your learning (e.g., science clubs, language clubs, or literary organizations).

☐ Study about fascinating places to travel. Gather information, and go there!

Applying Intellection Strengths in Academics

These insights and action ideas can help you apply Intellection strengths to achieve in various aspects of your academic life.

General Academic Life

☐ Ask questions and seek answers in discussions and lectures.

☐ Research subjects that interest and intrigue you.

☐ Contemplate academic goals and endeavors.

☐ Strengthen your education through your curiosity. The benefits you receive from the classes you take, the subject you major in, the way you study, and the way you approach a writing assignment will be increased when you ask questions.

Study Techniques

- ☐ Take time to think and plan before writing a paper or doing an assignment.
- ☐ Study to understand and learn, not just to memorize.
- ☐ Take part in study groups to verbalize and further define your thoughts.
- ☐ Practice presenting ideas that matter to you.

Relationships

- ☐ Get to know your professors, and engage in discussions with them.
- ☐ Try to meet people who share the same interests, and create intellectual conversations.
- ☐ Surround yourself with intellectually stimulating people, but be confident. You can contribute to their lives as well as they can to yours.

Class Selection

- ☐ Take classes that promote intellectual and analytical thought.
- ☐ Choose professors whose reputations indicate that they demand careful thinking.
- ☐ Study course syllabi to know how much thinking you might have an opportunity to do.

Extracurricular Activities

- ☐ Join clubs that allow you to be part of stimulating conversations.
- ☐ Read and collect books that pique your curiosity.
- ☐ Attend conferences and debates about subjects you are passionate about.

Applying Learner Strengths in Academics

These insights and action ideas can help you apply Learner strengths to achieve in various aspects of your academic life.

General Academic Life

- ☐ Keep a journal in which you reflect on what you learned from an experience or class.

- ☐ Read outside material that is related to your courses. This will not only impress the professor, it will help you develop a better understanding of the subject.

- ☐ Go over the limits. Do more than what the syllabus asks you to do.

- ☐ Look at every situation as a possible learning experience and use this to become aware of what you do well and where you need help.

- ☐ Always think, "What did I learn from this?"

Study Techniques

- ☐ Join study groups that are challenging for you.

- ☐ Study in an environment that allows you to get into a "study mood." This will allow you to get the most out of your studying.

- ☐ Figure out questions to ask, and practice answering them in preparation for discussions and exams.

- ☐ Treasure your capacity to concentrate. Do not let others distract you.

Relationships

- ☐ Identify other people and classmates who share your thirst for knowledge.

- ☐ Hang out with peers who are also motivated to learn.

- ☐ Have lots of conversations on subjects you are passionate about with people who are interested in learning.

- ☐ Build relationships with those from whom you want to learn.

Class Selection

☐ Choose challenging courses that will broaden your intellect.

☐ Enroll in college honors and departmental honors classes.

☐ Take classes that are particularly interesting to you.

Extracurricular Activities

☐ Choose jobs on campus that will provide learning experiences (for example, working for a professor).

☐ Engage in activities in which you can expand your knowledge about a subject you feel passionate about. Don't restrict your learning experiences to the classroom.

☐ Find opportunities to work with faculty and teaching assistants to make your college experience more meaningful. It will deepen your understanding of intellectual topics, concepts, and principles.

Applying Maximizer Strengths in Academics

These insights and action ideas can help you apply Maximizer strengths to achieve in various aspects of your academic life.

General Academic Life

☐ Consider specialized programs that allow you to practice your strengths.

☐ Find mentors and be one.

☐ Study success! Find out what made famous scientists, historic figures, and great innovators successful. The greatest outcome of college can be your insights into what makes people, societies, cultures, and groups successful.

☐ Select a college or university that offers leadership opportunities in which you can maximize the talents of others.

Study Techniques

☐ Read wherever you feel most comfortable — the library, the coffee shop, or home.

☐ Discover your best way to learn and stick to it.

☐ Determine ways to manage any weaknesses in your study habits.

☐ Study the most of what you do the best.

Relationships

☐ Help others use their strengths to the fullest.

☐ Help your friends recognize the talents and strengths in others.

☐ Associate with people who appreciate their strengths as well yours.

☐ Meet regularly with mentors and role models for insight, advice, and inspiration.

Class Selection

☐ Select elective courses that will provide opportunities to develop new strengths and hone your existing strengths.

☐ Choose your major on the basis of your greatest areas of talent and your personal mission. In what area of study do you have the greatest potential for strengths?

☐ Seek classes taught by professors whose teaching styles best match the way you learn.

Extracurricular Activities

☐ Find an internship or a job in which you can use your strengths.

☐ Involve yourself in mentoring or tutoring.

☐ Join organizations and clubs with missions related to development.

Applying Positivity Strengths in Academics

These insights and action ideas can help you apply Positivity strengths to achieve in various aspects of your academic life.

General Academic Life

☐ Help make learning fun.

☐ Share praise when appropriate.

☐ Help classmates laugh and relax when needed.

☐ Contribute to exciting class discussions.

Study Techniques

☐ Invite study partners who are as upbeat as you.

☐ Encourage others to enjoy their assignments.

☐ Think of fun, even silly, ways to remember things.

☐ Make learning fun for yourself and others by throwing study parties.

Relationships

☐ Express your positive attitudes about life to others.

☐ Transfer your energy into everything that you do.

☐ Let positivity reign, and avoid those who are guided by negative, destructive, and defeating attitudes and practices.

☐ Choose friends who love life as much as you do.

Class Selection

☐ Take classes that you find exciting and meaningful.

☐ Select courses where the professor is positive.

☐ Investigate what others with Positivity say about the course.

Extracurricular Activities

☐ Play team sports where you enjoy cheering others on.

☐ Be active in extracurricular activities that are fun for you.

☐ Pump energy into clubs you join.

Applying Relator Strengths in Academics

These insights and action ideas can help you apply Relator strengths to achieve in various aspects of your academic life.

General Academic Life

☐ Exchange phone numbers with classmates in case of absence.

☐ Create various lines of communication (i.e., verbal, phone, and e-mail) with friends in your classes.

☐ Seek out advisors, counselors, and professors who demonstrate genuine interest in you as a person.

☐ Seek out fellow students with whom you can play a mutual tutoring, learning assistance, and support role.

Study Techniques

☐ Form study groups for midterms and exams with close friends.

☐ Discuss class lectures with friends.

☐ Study with friends who have similar goals to yours.

☐ To increase your comprehension of reading materials, share what you have learned with friends.

Relationships

☐ Share knowledge with others and build a support network.

☐ Become a mentor and always have a mentor.

☐ Get to know professors who take an interest in you. Their involvement in your college experience will create a sense of belonging and stimulate your intellectual development as well as your academic achievement.

☐ Develop a college lifestyle through which you share your academic progress and performance with people who care about you, people both inside and outside the college environment.

Class Selection

☐ Choose classes where you have at least met the professor.

☐ Choose classes that friends are taking.

☐ Select classes that encourage friendships and belonging.

Extracurricular Activities

☐ Become involved in campus organizations that foster friendships.

☐ Join organizations that your friends and you have agreed upon.

☐ Consider community and humanitarian work that you can rally your close friends to be a part of too.

Applying Responsibility Strengths in Academics

These insights and action ideas can help you apply Responsibility strengths to achieve in various aspects of your academic life.

General Academic Life

☐ Prepare for the term by listing the dates of all tests, projects, and papers.

☐ Ask professors and successful students to show you what an "A" paper and an "A" essay look like.

☐ Think about what it would mean to be a truly responsible student. Work toward that standard in a progressive manner, taking one step at a time.

☐ Strive to always work ahead. Read ahead and work problems before the professor has presented them in class.

Study Techniques

☐ Discover what "doing it right" means to each of your professors.

☐ Schedule specific study times for each class, and assume the responsibility to invest the time necessary.

☐ Highlight items that you are responsible for in tests (i.e., vocabulary words, main ideas, characters).

☐ Make choices about class assignments as soon as possible.

Relationships

☐ Choose friends you trust.

☐ Find a mentor.

☐ Consider having a circle of friends who are older than you.

Class Selection

☐ Choose core classes or those required by your major first.

☐ Select professors you trust.

☐ Opt for courses in which you have choices to make about your learning.

Extracurricular Activities

☐ Wisely consider how much time you can devote to clubs and activities.

☐ Run for an office only if you have the capacity to fulfill it as you would like.

☐ Select organizations that stand for the same values you do.

Applying Restorative Strengths in Academics

These insights and action ideas can help you apply Restorative strengths to achieve in various aspects of your academic life.

General Academic Life

☐ Grow from your weaknesses. Don't get down on yourself for failing in certain areas.

☐ Read the syllabus when you get it, and attack assignments or areas that you consider problematic.

☐ Do not let an unexpectedly low grade defeat your spirits.

☐ Think about school as a way to improve yourself. This will increase your motivation, particularly if you reflect on your progress.

Study Techniques

☐ Make a list of ways that you can improve in each class.

☐ Ask your professors what your biggest weaknesses are.

☐ Research every missed question on tests.

☐ Insist that your friends help you to know your gaps in knowledge in your classes.

Relationships

☐ Let others know that you enjoy fixing their problems.

☐ Ask friends for honest feedback about your weaknesses.

☐ Build relationships with people who appreciate your ability to help them identify problems.

Class Selection

☐ Select classes where case solutions are emphasized.

☐ Select classes in which you learn to solve problems.

☐ Choose classes where the professor wants to fix things.

Extracurricular Activities

☐ Raise money for the disadvantaged.

☐ Organize a club that tackles and solves social issues on campus.

☐ Join an organization where you can restore something to its original condition.

Applying Self-Assurance Strengths in Academics

These insights and action ideas can help you apply Self-Assurance strengths to achieve in various aspects of your academic life.

General Academic Life

☐ Ensure that you are completely in control of your grades. Understand clearly what is expected and how to achieve.

☐ Always strive to become a better student. Stick with what is working for you and continue to build on those things.

☐ Be confident in your abilities to understand and learn material.

☐ Register for classes you are excited about.

Study Techniques

☐ Overstudy. Do more than you need to do.

☐ Have confidence in your best ways to learn.

☐ Study your talents and strengths, and recognize the many ways in which you can achieve through them.

☐ Enjoy the risks you take in your study life.

Relationships

☐ Get to know your professors and teaching assistants. This will help you stay in control of your learning.

☐ Build a friendship with an instructor that will last through your lifetime.

☐ Seek others who appreciate your self-confidence.

Class Selection

☐ Choose classes that you will find challenging and intriguing.

☐ Select classes that play to your strengths.

☐ Choose classes where you can claim a major success.

Extracurricular Activities

☐ Seek a leadership position in an organization that addresses issues that are important to you. You know you can make an impact on these issues.

☐ Join clubs that will "stretch" your strengths. Dare to tackle the unfamiliar.

☐ Consider a semester abroad. Your Self-Assurance will help you maneuver through a culture that is quite different from your own.

Applying Significance Strengths in Academics

These insights and action ideas can help you apply Significance strengths to achieve in various aspects of your academic life.

General Academic Life

☐ Think about why a particular class is important to your future .

☐ Identify three of your personal goals and connect them to your academic life.

☐ Take control of your life by starting with learning.

☐ Create a list of goals that will bring you great satisfaction in your personal life. Then, consider how college and learning can help you reach those goals.

Study Techniques

☐ Take a leadership role in a study group.

☐ Choose to study with other hard-charging classmates.

☐ Collect fans who help you finish your assignments.

☐ Establish relationships with your professors so they know who you are and of your interest in achieving.

Relationships

☐ Associate with professors and students who have similar aspirations or who are living out the desires you have. Connect with people who enhance your strengths and desires.

☐ You want people to know who you are. Become friends with people in your classes by initiating conversations with them even though it may be uncomfortable.

☐ You want people to appreciate your work, but if appreciation is not shown, don't give up — work even harder.

Class Selection

☐ Choose classes that offer you some independence.

☐ Select classes relevant to your goals and desires.

☐ Select classes in which you can be highly successful.

Extracurricular Activities

☐ Take part in activities that display your confidence — make public appearances, climb mountains.

☐ Be known for doing something excellently. Even if it is simple, just be better at doing it.

☐ Run for an elected office.

Applying Strategic Strengths in Academics

These insights and action ideas can help you apply Strategic strengths to achieve in various aspects of your academic life.

General Academic Life

☐ Don't be afraid to be different. Discuss with professors the various approaches you can take to tackle an assignment.

☐ Participate in research, or develop your own research project.

☐ Search for ways to express your creative thinking.

☐ Opt for classes that encourage discussion and creative solutions.

Study Techniques

☐ Reflect and write down your ideas for possible solutions to problems.

☐ Work in groups to generate new ideas and clarify or build on those you create.

☐ Be creative in your studying. Make up games or develop mnemonic devices and anecdotes to relate information.

☐ Do more than expected. It is not difficult for you to expand on an idea, and you will learn more about the subject.

Relationships

☐ Work with groups, and assume a leadership role in the group. You see the future more clearly than many.

☐ Select patterns that best achieve your leadership goals (always have your followers in mind).

☐ Encourage friends to call on you to devise the best way to achieve their goals.

Class Selection

☐ Take an independent-study class. Your Strategic strengths can help you work on your own.

☐ Consider elective classes with subject matter that lends itself to strategic thinking, like engineering or marketing.

☐ Choose classes that emphasize alternative ideas or solutions.

Extracurricular Activities

☐ Consider running for an elected office, and confidently state your ideas.

☐ Participate in cultural activities and exchanges to better understand the world around you.

☐ Find organizations that need your planning abilities.

Applying Woo Strengths in Academics

These insights and action ideas can help you apply Woo strengths to achieve in various aspects of your academic life.

General Academic Life

☐ Make classroom discussions fun by using words that catch the attention of others.

☐ Meet and greet the people in your classes.

☐ Use your charm when asking difficult questions in class.

Study Techniques

- ☐ Study in places where there are many people, like the library or an off-campus bookstore.

- ☐ Block off time for studying and reading with others.

- ☐ Connect reading material to people you have met. This helps you get involved in the reading and not become bored. Also, this helps you to better remember what you read and generate more insights.

- ☐ Create a study group of people you do not know yet.

Relationships

- ☐ Schedule a time (at least twice a quarter) when you visit your professors during office hours. Have them get to know you by name.

- ☐ Start a conversation with your classmates to identify students with whom you can work, learn, and study.

- ☐ Use your networking strengths every way you can. Prepare for class, exams, discussions, and papers with other people.

- ☐ Join social groups and study groups.

Class Selection

- ☐ Try to meet the professors before choosing classes.

- ☐ Choose classes that give you the opportunity to meet lots of people.

- ☐ Check in with those you know to learn about classes.

Extracurricular Activities

- ☐ Get involved in an activity or group that gives you the opportunity to connect with different people.

- ☐ Balance your academics with extracurricular activities to keep yourself involved with people.

- ☐ Run for an elected office. A person with strong Woo can quickly connect with people and create positive reactions.

- ☐ Chair large social events. Turn on your charm to engage others.

Chapter IX

BECOMING YOUR OWN BEST EDUCATOR AND LEARNER

For more than 30 years, Professor Robert Rosenthal has conducted experiments on the power of expectations to influence performance and intellectual competence. Here is a summary of one of his most famous experiments.

Oak School is a public elementary school with approximately 650 students. At the beginning of one school year, all of the students were pre-tested with a standard test of intelligence. The teachers were told that the test could predict "intellectual blooming" and also predict which students would soon experience "spurts" of intellectual development.

About 20% of the Oak School students were identified as "potential bloomers." Each of the 18 teachers was given the names of those "special" students in his or her class who would show dramatic intellectual growth in the academic year ahead. These predictions were allegedly made on the basis of these "special" students' scores on the test for potential "academic blooming."

However, the "special" students had actually been chosen randomly. The difference between them and the "ordinary" students was only in the minds of the teachers.

All of the Oak School students were retested with the same intelligence test after one semester and again at the end of the year.

When the test scores of the "special" students and the "ordinary" students were calculated, both groups showed an improvement in total I.Q., verbal I.Q., and reasoning I.Q. But when the two groups were compared, 47% of the "special" students had gained 20 or more total I.Q. points, while only 19% of the "ordinary" students gained 20 or more total I.Q. points.

The Power of Expectations

Research by Dr. Rosenthal and others clearly indicates that our expectations have a powerful effect on ourselves and others. These expectations influence our actions, attitudes, motivation, and perseverance. In fact, they influence every aspect of achieving, including whether or not we will even enter into activities where we can achieve excellence. Because of the critical importance of expectations, we want you to consider these questions.

1. Why do you think the "special" students at Oak School performed so well?

2. If these "special" students had the ability to achieve such excellence all along, why hadn't they performed as well before?

3. If these teachers were able to promote achievement among "special" students at this level, what would happen if they thought all of their students were "special"?

4. Are there certain people who you think are "special"? If so, what expectations do you have of them?

5. In what ways do your expectations of these "special" people influence their achievements and performance?

6. In what ways do you think you are "special" and have real potential for blossoming?

7. In what ways are your self-expectations encouraging your achievements and performance?

The Missed Opportunities Revealed by Rosenthal's Research

Dr. Rosenthal's research has been very helpful in improving how teachers are trained and the expectations they have of themselves, their roles, and their interactions with students. But this research also shines a light on what we believe is a series of key points.

The first key point is that the "special" students always had the ability to blossom, but no one ever brought that ability to the surface. If the "special" students wouldn't have had the ability before the school year began, no amount of good teaching could have produced results that were more than double what the "ordinary" students achieved.

The second key point is that it took fraudulent information from a researcher to get the teachers to help their students blossom. The teachers already had the ability to produce academic achievements among their students. The teachers were not given any different curriculum, nor were they given any additional teaching methods, training, or new technology. Sadly, although these teachers already had within them the ability to inspire students to blossom, they had not put that ability to use.

The third key point revealed by Rosenthal's research was that the underperformance by both the students and the teachers stemmed from the teachers' "ordinary" expectations of their "ordinary" students. Just think about all of the students at Oak School who did not achieve their potential because their teachers didn't see them as being anything special. The sad thing about this is that normal expectations are usually low.

Some students experience only negative expectations every day. Some of these negative expectations are placed arbitrarily on young people simply because of how they look, their gender, socio-economic status, or ethnicity.

A great deal of research is now being conducted about the topic of "stereotype threat." This research shows that when people are in an environment where they perceive that they are being stereotyped with negative expectations about their abilities to perform, their performances confirm the negative expectations, like self-fulfilling prophecies. Research by Stanford University Professor Claude Steele and others reveals that environmental expectations form and reinforce self-expectations that directly influence performance.

What Really Happened in the Rosenthal Studies of Expectations?

The teachers in Rosenthal's study acted differently toward the "special" students, both in how they taught and in how they interacted with these students. In essence, the experimenters had changed the teachers' approaches to their students by manipulating the teachers' perceptions of the students.

More than 400 studies have been conducted to document the powerful effects of expectations. Drs. Rosenthal and Monica Harris have synthesized the research findings from many of these studies to determine exactly what teachers do when they are given more favorable information about certain "high potential" students. What follows is a list of the teachers' behaviors toward the students who they were told had special abilities and special potential for achieving.

1. Teachers expressed more positive attitudes, behaviors, and emotional warmth toward the "special" students.

2. Teachers more frequently acknowledged, applied, and/or summarized what the "special" students had to say.

3. Teachers taught the "special" students more challenging material than they presented to the "normal" students.

4. Teachers interacted with the "special" students more frequently about both academic and nonacademic topics.

5. Teachers made eye contact with the "special" students more frequently.

6. Teachers asked the "special" students more questions.

7. Teachers gave the "special" students more positive feedback and praise.

A Radical Idea: Become Your Own Best Teacher

Dr. Winston C. Doby has conceptualized a learning system based on a group of beliefs found among outstanding learners. In particular, he has found that top learners believe they are their own best teachers and take personal responsibility for their own learning.

Quite often, an ineffective relationship between a teacher and a learner is the result of miscommunication or a lack of communication. But when you are your own teacher and your own learner, there is very little chance of these communication problems. Your inner dialogue and your clear self-awareness are primary reasons why you can be your own best teacher and your own best learner. Also, the basis for your positive expectations about yourself is neither random nor fraudulent. You know you have talents of great value.

We challenge you to be at least as good with your "student within" as the teachers in Rosenthal's study were with their special students.

Putting this in practical terms, consider doing the following.

1. Express positive attitudes toward yourself as a learner.

2. Use challenging material to encourage growth.

3. Give positive feedback and praise to your learner within.

Know this: If you want to achieve excellence in education, you must assume the responsibility of being your own best teacher and your own best learner.

Perception of Talent

Perception of talent plays an extremely influential role in a person's motivation to achieve.

When people perceive that they have few talents, they usually avoid any activity that may reveal that lack of talent. Procrastination is a typical manifestation of a perceived lack of talent. It's like a game in which you do everything at the last minute so that if you don't succeed, you can blame the failure on a lack of time rather than a lack of talent.

In our experience, most people perceive that they have very few, if any, talents. And even when people are aware of their talents, they aren't very clear about the nature of their talents or what to do with them. They also tend to believe that their talents have limited uses and are applicable in only one or two areas.

People may even totally misperceive a talent, thinking it is a weakness.

We emphasize the "perception" of talent because when people decide to enter or avoid an achievement activity, they are not making their decision based on what their talents really are or what they are actually capable of doing through them. They make their achievement or avoidance decision on the basis of their perception of their talents.

Becoming Your Own Best Educator and Learner

It has been said that there is no lasting change without a change of identity. Your identity is your perception of who you are, and it forms the boundaries of what you attempt to do. People seldom undertake tasks beyond their perception of who they are and what they can do.

Earlier in this chapter, we presented the radical idea that you are your own best teacher. This idea by Dr. Doby is similar to Parker Palmer's concept of the educator within. We would like to take these ideas to a higher level and encourage you to pursue a greater identity: *You are your own best educator and learner.*

Never forget that we live in a fast-moving world in which only three things are certain: (1) rapid change, (2) continuing knowledge explosion, and (3) increasingly complex relationships that are more difficult to maintain. To cope, let alone achieve in this environment, everyone faces the possibility of becoming "obsolete" if they don't keep learning.

Lifelong learning isn't a luxury; it's a necessity. Being a lifelong learner is your only way of coping with rapid change, knowledge explosion, and complex relationships. No matter what field you enter, you must forever be a learner, or you will get left behind.

What the Very Best Educators Do

First and foremost, great educators see the potential for growth within learners. They see the talents of learners, and they recognize the great potential for strengths. They don't have a "fix-it" attitude, but a growth attitude. When educators see potential for growth, they feel compelled to stimulate and facilitate growth in the learners. It is as if they can't help themselves.

Now, be sure to apply this as you think of yourself as your own best educator and learner.

The very best educators are mission driven. They take great satisfaction from the growth they see in their learners. Once again, we want you to be this type of educator for yourself. We want you to recognize and celebrate your progress as a learner.

Do you have a mission to fully develop your talents into strengths? Do you have a sense of vision about the importance of what you could do when you reach your potential? If so, you will experience great satisfaction as you see your own best educator helping your own best learner reach his or her potential.

Chapter X

STRENGTHS AND CAREER PLANNING

Mark Twain told the story of a man who searched his whole life for the world's greatest general. When the man died, he arrived in heaven and walked up to St. Peter and said, "I'm looking for the world's greatest general."

St. Peter replied, "I know. We've been expecting you, and I have good news. If you will look right over there, you will see the world's greatest general."

The older man excitedly looked over and said, "That's not the world's greatest general. That man was a cobbler on Main Street in my hometown."

St. Peter responded, "But had he been a general, he would have been the greatest general ever."

This story is not meant to demean cobblers at all. The work of a cobbler is meaningful and requires very special talents. But the story does raise some fundamental questions: Did the cobbler know what he had the potential to do? Did he know that he had the talent to be the world's greatest general? Did anyone try to convince him that he could be destined for greatness?

Twain's tale hints at a painful truth: There are plenty of perfectly good cobblers out there who could have been great generals, given the opportunity or encouragement. Maybe, given the choice, they would still have chosen to be cobblers. But they also could have pursued completely different, perhaps historic, careers. Give this tale some thought when planning your own career.

If You Are Struggling With Career Planning, You Are Not Alone.

Don't let anyone ever tell you that career planning is easy. It's one of the most difficult, frustrating, and overwhelming experiences you will go through. Many people avoid it for as long as possible. Others simply accept the first career that presents itself. Still others avoid turmoil by going into whatever career they think their parents might like them to pursue.

We will show you how your talents and strengths relate to careers. We will also give you some practical suggestions about how to plan a successful and fulfilling career. But first, we want to reassure you that the process of career planning is a challenge for everyone — if you are struggling, you are not alone.

What Makes Career Planning So Difficult?

1. Career planning challenges you to predict the future.

Career planning involves setting a direction for your life's work. But is that even possible? Is it possible to select a career today that will be rewarding, fulfilling, and meaningful 5, 10, 15, 20, or more years from now?

2. Career planning makes you question who you will be.

The world around us is always changing, and so are we. Go back in your mind 5 or 10 years and think about who you were then in contrast to who you are now. What did you think was important then, and what is important to you now? What activities did you enjoy then, but don't enjoy now?

3. Career planning challenges you to come to grips with your ultimate values.

Your career represents far more than your work, income, security, and benefits. Your career will be one of the most important factors in determining your entire way of life. It will directly impact how much time you spend with your family, where you live, how often you move, who your friends are, and how much freedom and flexibility you have.

4. Career planning forces you to come to conclusions about who you think you are and what you believe about your talents and potential.

It would be terribly misguided to go into a career where you have no ability to excel and no capacity to develop the skills to be competent. Therefore, the career-planning process forces you to take a close look at yourself. You must identify the areas of talent in which you have the greatest potential for growth and strength.

5. At times, some people think it is their right and responsibility to give you "advice" about the career you should enter.

It is hard enough to recognize your own values, interests, and talents. Input from others is valuable, but when people believe they must press on you their own values, interests, and opinions — essentially directing you into the career of their choice — the task becomes much more difficult.

6. **Career planning challenges you to come to grips with philosophical and theological issues.**

Some of the great existential issues involve finding and creating meaning in life. There are personality theories that emphasize our desire and search for meaning. Other theorists emphasize a search for the inner experience of vitality and point to a *carpe diem*, or "seize the day," perspective. Some religions teach that there is a divine plan or purpose for every individual. Each of these philosophical and theological issues has a direct bearing on career planning and presents yet another level of complexity.

7. **Career planning involves a "cost-benefit" analysis of your time, energy, and resources.**

Part of the career-planning process involves looking at the costs and benefits of entering various careers. But it isn't quite as easy as that because the *actual* costs may be greater than you anticipate, and the *actual benefits* may never materialize. Realistically, we are looking at *anticipated* costs and *presumed* benefits. The unpredictability of the costs and the uncertainty of the benefits are part of what makes career planning so difficult.

Strengths and the World of Work

The world of work is a big one, so let's break it down and consider the relationships between its various aspects and the concept of strengths.

1. Strengths and service or volunteer work

Service or volunteer work — that is, unpaid and often charitable work — provides training, instruction, and feedback to help you develop strengths that you may want to eventually use in a paid position. Many people apply some of their finest strengths in performing service or volunteer work.

2. Strengths and jobs

A job — paid work that involves minimal long-term commitment, as distinct from a career — can provide outstanding opportunities to discover talents, develop them into strengths, and apply those strengths. Part-time and full-time jobs provide rich sources of information about what you do best, what you enjoy doing, and what types of tasks you learn quickly. As you begin recognizing your talents, you can also begin to consider potential jobs on the basis of the strengths-development opportunities they would provide.

3. Strengths and careers

For many, one's career — to which a long-term commitment is made — and one's life are inseparable. Undoubtedly, you want to have a career in which you can achieve, succeed, and excel. And if this is true, you must make sure that you select a career in which you can develop and apply strengths.

4. Strengths and professions

Everything stated about careers also applies to professions, but the stakes are higher. Professions — such as law, medicine, or academics — require advanced degrees. So, you don't want to invest energy and money in years of education, only to wake up one day and say, "This profession just doesn't fit me!"

5. Strengths and vocation

Many people believe that God or some "higher power" calls them to fulfill a general or specific plan. Some just feel the whisper of inspiration from deep within themselves. Sometimes, the calling is to a specific form of ministry or service. But a vocation is different in that it doesn't have to be specific to a particular role, career, or type of volunteer work. The focus of vocation is in responding to a powerful sense of mission and purpose.

Organizing Principles for Strengths-Based Career Planning

There aren't any simple formulas, tests, or computer inventories that will tell you exactly which career will be the most fulfilling for you. There are, however, a group of principles that can guide your thinking and decision-making.

1. **Your starting point and primary focus in career planning should be yourself, rather than the career.**

There are over 100,000 careers, professions, and career specializations.

If you start by focusing on all of your career options, you'll surely feel overwhelmed. But even more important, by focusing first on careers, you leave out the single most important factor in career planning. And that is *you*.

2. Career planning begins by taking every important aspect of your inner life seriously.

For some, the inner life seems as confusing and overwhelming as the outer world. For others, the inner life seems like an unknowable "black box" of conflicting needs, desires, and motives. Still others are simply afraid of what they might find if they examine too closely what is within them.

We aren't interested in probing your inner life to discover what's "wrong" with you — just the opposite. We want to encourage you to see what's right with you. We want you to take seriously those most important and most precious parts of your identity, and then bring these aspects into the career- planning process.

3. In your talents, you already have within you the potential to achieve in several careers and professions.

You do not need to try to become someone else in order to achieve. Also, you don't have to worry about there being only one career in which you can achieve.

4. There isn't a "perfect" career, profession, or vocation that will fit you or all of your talents and strengths exactly.

This principle offers a dose of reality that many find difficult to accept. We might like to think that there is some career out there that will fit us perfectly. But we don't know of any cases where that is true. However, there are many careers that will allow you to develop and apply a great number of strengths.

Our studies of the top achievers in most careers and professions indicate that top achievers "invent" ways to develop and apply their strengths as they work. If they can't, they move on until they find a career in which they can.

Career Implications of Your Strengths

Now, it's time to check out your final set of strategies. These particular strategies were created to help you consider careers that could best match strengths you now or may someday possess within your Signature Themes. Please locate and examine the strategies that are customized to your Signature Themes. As you think them over, keep in mind that all of our strategies are only a beginning. You certainly will be able to think of additional ways that your greatest talents can be developed into strengths you can use to produce success in careers and all other aspects of your life.

Applying Your Strengths in Careers

Applying Achiever Strengths in Careers

These observations and suggestions will help you consider careers that could best suit Achiever strengths. As you think them over, select those that apply to you best.

☐ Choose work environments that challenge you. Opt for situations where your success is measured each day.

☐ Select a career that provides you with numerous opportunities to excel as an individual. Control your workflow, schedule, productivity, quality level, and action plan.

☐ Gravitate to organizations and professions that offer incentives for quality, productivity, sales revenue, profit margins, or customer service.

☐ Seek a position that lets you do what you do best every day. Inform people that you have a need to exceed, not just meet, minimum requirements.

☐ Find a career in which you can work as hard as you want. Avoid work situations controlled by collective bargaining agreements that limit how much you can produce each day.

☐ Realize that you cannot work in just anywhere. Affiliate yourself with organizations that are known for their serious, results-oriented workers.

Applying Activator Strengths in Careers

These observations and suggestions will help you consider careers that could best suit Activator strengths. As you think them over, select those that apply to you best.

☐ Define what kind of leader you are. A thought leader? A giver of orders? A leader who gives the go-ahead signal? Large group leader? Small group leader? A leader with a mission? A profit leader? An athlete leader?

☐ Identify informal leadership roles within professions, companies, or departments into which you can step. Persuade coworkers that they can increase productivity, solve problems, launch programs, overcome obstacles, and bounce back from defeat.

☐ Find work that allows you to make your own decisions, and then act upon them.

☐ Consider becoming your own boss. Make of list of possible businesses you could start, grow, and sell once they show a profit. Understand that you will probably lose interest once an enterprise is so fine-tuned that it runs on its own. Recall how maintaining an operation has led to boredom in the past.

☐ Choose a career in which "actions speak louder than words" even though your words can propel people into action. Thoroughly research professions, organizations, and companies to identify the ones that are truly results-oriented.

☐ Understand that some supervisors and managers may feel threatened by your insistence on making decisions and acting without delay.

Applying Adaptability Strengths in Careers

These observations and suggestions will help you consider careers that could best suit Adaptability strengths. As you think them over, select those that apply to you best.

☐ Identify three to four occupations that reward those with an ability to live in the moment. Avoid professions that require rigid adherence to rules, operating procedures, and time controls.

☐ Interview individuals who work in organizations where the work is experimental or discovery-oriented. Ask how each day assumes its own life. Take notes. Afterwards, look for recurring themes and behaviors these people share.

☐ Gain part-time or seasonal employment in organizations where the demand for flexibility exists hour-by-hour and day-by-day. Record three to five ways your Adaptability talent benefits you in these settings.

☐ Reflect upon "wrong fit" jobs you have had in the past. Determine whether your Adaptability talent was viewed as a plus or as a liability. What did these experiences teach you?

☐ Start a "right fit" career file. Each week, add an insight about how you used your Adaptability talent. Draw upon this information when writing résumés and preparing for job interviews.

☐ Shadow employees who continually respond to the varied requests of their customers, tourists, guests, and patients.

Applying Analytical Strengths in Careers

These observations and suggestions will help you consider careers that could best suit Analytical strengths. As you think them over, select those that apply to you best.

☐ Choose a job that requires a lot of analysis. Obvious career fields such as accounting, finance, law, engineering, sciences, business management, computer technology, and journalism are worthy of consideration.

☐ Opt for jobs that allow you to make decisions based on your evaluation of facts, data, tangible evidence, circumstantial evidence, and research findings.

☐ Examine the use of logic in fields such as history, theater, painting, landscape design, anthropology, auto mechanics, and musical composition.

☐ Refuse to sacrifice your passion for a field because others say it does not require linear, sequential thinking. Prove them wrong.

☐ Select careers that permit you to sharpen your ability to determine the existence of cause-and-effect relationships on a daily basis.

☐ Decline opportunities to do mindless work regardless of the compensation and benefits package offered to you.

Applying Arranger Strengths in Careers

These observations and suggestions will help you consider careers that could best suit Arranger strengths. As you think them over, select those that apply to you best.

☐ Explore careers that demand constant readjustment. Determine how much change and what kinds of changes you are most comfortable handling.

☐ Weigh the importance of rules and guidelines in your job. Understand that abiding by these makes it easier for teammates to cooperate, make progress, and succeed.

☐ For an interesting and challenging project, enlist friends and classmates to search the Internet for information about team-oriented occupations.

☐ Look through the classified ads for positions that allow you to help others meet their financial obligations.

☐ Identify jobs in which you will be expected to put together pieces of plans, processes, projects, and events.

☐ Consider being an agent of change. Interview individuals who regularly turn around bad situations by redeploying resources, readjusting timelines, and realigning priorities. Ask them how they know it is time for them to move on to another role.

Applying Belief Strengths in Careers

These observations and suggestions will help you consider careers that could best suit Belief strengths. As you think them over, select those that apply to you best.

☐ Turn down high-paying jobs that force you to compromise your beliefs. Tell the hiring officer that your soul and psyche are not for sale to the highest bidder.

☐ Seek employment in companies and organizations that exhibit a strong sense of mission — that is, a commitment to positively impacting the quality of people's lives.

☐ Compare an entity's mission statement to what it produces or the services it provides. Verify that its guiding principles and its outcomes are in sync.

☐ Research opportunities in helping professions such as medicine, law enforcement, social work, refugee relocation, teaching, and search-and-rescue. Talk with people who provide services to individuals in need. Interview those who supervise them.

☐ Have a mentor, and be a mentor. Understand that this increases the chances for your behaviors, decisions, and beliefs to remain constant.

☐ Consider an ethics-related career in medicine, law, military service, law enforcement, ministry, or science.

Applying Command Strengths in Careers

These observations and suggestions will help you consider careers that could best suit Command strengths. As you think them over, select those that apply to you best.

- ☐ Leverage your persuasiveness when choosing a career. Consider fields such as law, entrepreneurship, sales, politics, education, medicine, and ministry.

- ☐ Explore various opportunities in sales. Determine what kinds of products and services you would and would not enjoy selling.

- ☐ Aim to be in a managerial or authoritarian role. Remember, you tend to be bossy. Avoid occupations where you are expected to blindly follow orders or be subservient.

- ☐ Investigate careers that offer upward mobility. Understand that you are satisfied with a subordinate position for only a limited time.

- ☐ Assume a role that permits you to create and control your own and others' work.

- ☐ Use your air of certainty and boldness to calm coworkers in the midst of situations that confound and overwhelm them.

Applying Communication Strengths in Careers

These observations and suggestions will help you consider careers that could best suit Communication strengths. As you think them over, select those that apply to you best.

☐ Consider becoming a stand-up comedian, actor, motivational speaker, or trainer.

☐ Choose careers that will allow you to do a lot of the talking, such as teaching, broadcast journalism, consulting, politics, public relations, and ministry.

☐ Explore opportunities to serve as the spokesperson for an organization, product, political candidate, company, school district, hospital, or elected official.

☐ Become a librarian who reads stories to children.

☐ Opt for a career as a professional storyteller.

☐ Explore sales positions that require making presentations.

Applying Competition Strengths in Careers

These observations and suggestions will help you consider careers that could best suit Competition strengths. As you think them over, select those that apply to you best.

☐ Choose work environments that challenge you and in which your success can be quantified with scores, ratings, and rankings. Avoid situations lacking meaningful, objective measurement criteria.

☐ Decide whether you prefer to compete as an individual or as a team member. Select employment that matches your preference either for total or shared control over final results.

☐ Search for jobs that offer incentives for best performance. Financial bonuses, trophies, trips, promotions, rings, cars, or learning opportunities enhance your performance in ways that hard work and long hours cannot.

☐ Find a career that is both competitive and personally satisfying. Refuse to sacrifice one for the other.

Applying Connectedness Strengths in Careers

These observations and suggestions will help you consider careers that could best suit Connectedness strengths. As you think them over, select those that apply to you best.

☐ Dedicate at least two years of your life to serving your country or community after graduation. Join Volunteers in Service to America (VISTA), AmeriCorps, or Teach for America.

☐ Incorporate your need to serve all of humankind into whatever career you choose. Opt to work in fields and for organizations whose values mirror your own.

☐ Enlist in the Peace Corps before starting your professional career.

☐ Volunteer your medical services for a week or month at a rural clinic serving migrant workers or in a small town without a physician or nurse.

☐ Consider joining Doctors Without Borders® or becoming a medical missionary.

☐ Make a lifetime commitment to a specific ministry within your faith tradition.

Applying Consistency Strengths in Careers

These observations and suggestions will help you consider careers that could best suit Consistency strengths. As you think them over, select those that apply to you best.

☐ Work in environments that have regulations, policies, procedures, and guidelines firmly established. Realize that you are more effective and efficient when everyone, regardless of status, must follow the same rules.

☐ Gravitate to careers in fields such as accounting, tax law, manufacturing, and government service.

☐ Research roles in quality assurance, risk management, safety compliance, law enforcement, and production standards.

☐ Consider refereeing athletic events.

☐ Choose workplaces where standard operating procedures are emphasized in orientation, training, development, and manuals.

☐ Explore positions where careful monitoring of the bidding process, contract specifications, and open meetings laws are critical to success.

Applying Context Strengths in Careers

These observations and suggestions will help you consider careers that could best suit Context strengths. As you think them over, select those that apply to you best.

☐ Consider a career as a teacher, archivist, museum curator, documentary filmmaker, journalist, or fiction writer. Or, consider archeology, anthropology, reclamation of sunken ships, or reconstruction of historic sites. Concentrate on a particular period or figure in history.

☐ Specialize in genealogy. Help people trace their family's lineage for purposes of membership in an organization or to prove their relationship for historic or legal purposes.

☐ Join the National Park Service and specialize in giving guided tours of historic sites. Oversee the ongoing maintenance of the property and its collection of artifacts and documents.

☐ Examine opportunities as an appraiser of antique furniture, toys, clothing, jewelry, paintings, first edition books, or original manuscripts. Study how individuals become partners in auction houses.

Applying Deliberative Strengths in Careers

These observations and suggestions will help you consider careers that could best suit Deliberative strengths. As you think them over, select those that apply to you best.

☐ Choose a career in which you and others can benefit from your careful thinking and deliberation.

☐ You may want to work in roles that require research and analysis of information to plan wise actions or gain new understandings.

☐ Work in organizations and roles in which you can be independent.

☐ You will be a good questioner of actions, helping others to think through their decisions before moving ahead too quickly.

Applying Developer Strengths in Careers

These observations and suggestions will help you consider careers that could best suit Developer strengths. As you think them over, select those that apply to you best.

☐ You will be most satisfied in a career that provides some type of service to people or in which organizational success is based on interpersonal relationships and your ability to help people be successful.

☐ Choose a job in which you work in teams or partnerships so that you can help others grow and develop.

☐ You will be an asset to any organization because you help facilitate the development of those around you. Never forget the impact that you can have in an organization.

☐ Consider a career in counseling, human resources, teaching, or management. You have a talent for noting people's progress and for helping them become even better at what they do.

Applying Discipline Strengths in Careers

These observations and suggestions will help you consider careers that could best suit Discipline strengths. As you think them over, select those that apply to you best.

- ☐ Take on a career in which you can maintain order for yourself and others.

- ☐ Your organizing skills should be helpful in administrative positions.

- ☐ Find jobs that require exactness.

- ☐ You will be appreciated in most work settings because you follow through and you work systematically.

- ☐ You can do a lot to help others become organized. This makes them become more effective and improves their follow through.

- ☐ In many ways you are a perfectionist. While some may criticize your perfectionism, just think of all the professions in which you wouldn't want someone who wasn't a perfectionist (e.g., airplane pilot, brain surgeon, accountant).

Applying Empathy Strengths in Careers

These observations and suggestions will help you consider careers that could best suit Empathy strengths. As you think them over, select those that apply to you best.

- ☐ Try to work in a peer counseling center or in a job where you give advice or are called to understand others.

- ☐ Look for a job in which you need to work as part of a team. You will understand team members, support them, and help them work together.

- ☐ Great teachers have been found to be especially high in the Empathy theme.

- ☐ Some outstanding writers are high in empathy.

- ☐ Listening is one of your greatest skills. By listening to the feelings of others, you help them become clearer and less conflicted.

Applying Focus Strengths in Careers

These observations and suggestions will help you consider careers that could best suit Focus strengths. As you think them over, select those that apply to you best.

☐ You will be most satisfied in a career that has identifiable goals, purposes, and objectives, and one that provides opportunities to meet your own longer-term goals.

☐ You will be helpful in an organization that will use your abilities to set goals and priorities.

☐ Because you are able to keep yourself on track, you will work best in an environment with minimal supervision.

☐ Set measurable steps for reaching your goals. These will help you track your progress toward your desired career.

Applying Futuristic Strengths in Careers

These observations and suggestions will help you consider careers that could best suit Futuristic strengths. As you think them over, select those that apply to you best.

- ☐ Dream big. Write down your dreams, and continue to make progress toward your biggest dreams.

- ☐ Find an organization where you can help create the future, painting vivid pictures for those who work there, helping them see the role they will take in making this vision become reality.

- ☐ Choose a career in which you can help others envision their future and define their goals to reach it.

- ☐ Choose jobs that will help you gain the connections you need for the job you want after graduation.

Applying Harmony Strengths in Careers

These observations and suggestions will help you consider careers that could best suit Harmony strengths. As you think them over, select those that apply to you best.

☐ Look for a career where you will have opportunities to be a stabilizing factor in a group, team, or organization.

☐ Avoid a career in which there is significant conflict.

☐ Seek out environments that provide security, compatibility, and low risk.

☐ You are practical, and all organizations need practical people to get the work done and keep the organization running. You can help others see the practical in the theoretical.

☐ You work well and are helpful in team project environments. You help others work together even more productively. You help promote emotional stability and calmness in the group.

Applying Ideation Strengths in Careers

These observations and suggestions will help you consider careers that could best suit Ideation strengths. As you think them over, select those that apply to you best.

- ☐ Build on your creativity to find a career that encourages you to think freely and express your ideas.
- ☐ Find work in which others like your ideas and in which you are expected to keep learning.
- ☐ You will be able to find new and better ways of doing things within the organization.
- ☐ Select an organization where the leaders encourage and solicit your divergent thinking, stimulating them to consider some new approaches.

Applying Includer Strengths in Careers

These observations and suggestions will help you consider careers that could best suit Includer strengths. As you think them over, select those that apply to you best.

- ☐ Choose a career where you can supervise or lead a group of people, because you will build a sense of team and belongingness.

- ☐ You will add benefit to a work environment, bringing them together for a common goal.

- ☐ Working with a group that is not always included by others, such as physically or mentally challenged children, will allow you to use your talents to help them feel better about themselves.

- ☐ A career in the United Nations or foreign service may appeal to you. You appreciate and include all people and their ideas.

- ☐ The field of social work may interest you. Making sure that children are placed in a home where they are loved and become a real part of the family would give you great pleasure.

Applying Individualization Strengths in Careers

These observations and suggestions will help you consider careers that could best suit Individualization strengths. As you think them over, select those that apply to you best.

☐ A career in education would directly use your talents because you would value and treat each student as an individual.

☐ As a supervisor or manager, you would help individuals determine what they could do what they do best on a regular basis. Your evaluations would be based on who the person is and on what he or she had accomplished.

☐ Counseling could be a fulfilling role for you. Your ability to see people as distinct individuals will empower them and help them grow.

☐ Writing a novel would allow you to fully develop the uniqueness of each character.

Applying Input Strengths in Careers

These observations and suggestions will help you consider careers that could best suit Input strengths. As you think them over, select those that apply to you best.

☐ You will want to work in an environment that expects you to be continuously engaged in learning.

☐ You will enjoy a career where you are always on the cutting edge of knowledge and where you are stimulated by ideas and creative approaches to problems and issues.

☐ An ideal career would be one in which you have an opportunity to share what you have learned and are expected to be continuously learning and making new discoveries.

☐ Choose jobs that will encourage you to conduct or delve into research.

☐ Being a media specialist or someone with access to large amounts of information that you can locate for people would be rewarding for you.

Applying Intellection Strengths in Careers

These observations and suggestions will help you consider careers that could best suit Intellection strengths. As you think them over, select those that apply to you best.

☐ Choose work that will challenge you intellectually.

☐ Choose a work environment that matches your most productive thinking environment. If you think best when it's quiet, choose a quiet work environment. If working with others stimulates your thinking, choose to work in a team environment.

☐ Select work where you can share ideas and pose questions.

☐ Look at careers in which you can interact with colleagues and have philosophical debates.

Applying Learner Strengths in Careers

These observations and suggestions will help you consider careers that could best suit Learner strengths. As you think them over, select those that apply to you best.

☐ Choose a work environment that encourages constant learning.

☐ Find work where study is a way of life.

☐ Consider work that allows you to move to the next subject that greatly interests you.

☐ Select work where competency is valued and where you will have opportunities to keep developing your competencies.

Applying Maximizer Strengths in Careers

These observations and suggestions will help you consider careers that could best suit Maximizer strengths. As you think them over, select those that apply to you best.

☐ Choose a career that allows you to improve on the qualities you already have.

☐ Don't hide your weaknesses in your work; just make them irrelevant by fully developing and applying your strengths.

☐ Find work where you can help others see their talents and how their talents make a difference.

☐ Choose a work environment where your talents will be appreciated.

Applying Positivity Strengths in Careers

These observations and suggestions will help you consider careers that could best suit Positivity strengths. As you think them over, select those that apply to you best.

☐ Select a fast-paced, stimulating work environment.

☐ Choose work for which you have passion.

☐ Choose a career where you can encourage others, like coaching, teaching, selling, or managing.

☐ Make sure any work you choose is fun for you.

Applying Relator Strengths in Careers

These observations and suggestions will help you consider careers that could best suit Relator strengths. As you think them over, select those that apply to you best.

☐ Choose any career in which in-depth, meaningful relationships are valued.

☐ Find a workplace in which friendships are encouraged, and you can continuously learn about your clients and associates.

☐ You will enjoy a job in which you serve a stable group of customers who come back often.

☐ Consider coaching, teaching, managing, supervising, and caregiving as possible outlets for your talent.

Applying Responsibility Strengths in Careers

These observations and suggestions will help you consider careers that could best suit Responsibility strengths. As you think them over, select those that apply to you best.

☐ Select work where you can be given more and more responsibility as you progressively achieve.

☐ Ensure that future employers know how much they can count on you.

☐ Choose a work environment that focuses on outcomes rather than processes.

☐ Find a manager and coworkers who will trust you to follow through.

Applying Restorative Strengths in Careers

These observations and suggestions will help you consider careers that could best suit Restorative strengths. As you think them over, select those that apply to you best.

☐ Choose a profession where deficits are remedied.

☐ Consider a service position where you can help others solve their problems.

☐ Look for work opportunities that allow you to fix whatever is wrong, from restoring art objects to cars to inadequate telephone service.

☐ Think about owning or managing a company that restores and re-cycles products.

Applying Self-Assurance Strengths in Careers

These observations and suggestions will help you consider careers that could best suit Self-Assurance strengths. As you think them over, select those that apply to you best.

☐ Find a career that will constantly challenge you and keep you motivated.

☐ Find a career in which you can practice all your talents and abilities and identify new ones.

☐ Choose a career where you are in control.

☐ Don't be afraid to trust your instincts and take risks in your career.

Applying Significance Strengths in Careers

These observations and suggestions will help you consider careers that could best suit Significance strengths. As you think them over, select those that apply to you best.

☐ Choose a career in which you can be looked up to or admired.

☐ Work with people who show that they appreciate your hard work.

☐ Choose a career that you think is very significant.

☐ Consider work that puts you in the public eye.

☐ Identify the strengths that will help you make an extraordinary contribution and/or achievement. Make others aware that receiving recognition that you deserve will motivate you to even greater contributions.

Applying Strategic Strengths in Careers

These observations and suggestions will help you consider careers that could best suit Strategic strengths. As you think them over, select those that apply to you best.

☐ Consider psychology, as it requires understanding situations and being able to discover or provide effective problem solving.

☐ A career in law may excite you, as it requires the use of logic to build cases and find creative and effective ways to present them.

☐ Choose careers that will allow you to be a leader and voice your ideas.

☐ List the various paths possible in your future so you can give careful thought to each one.

☐ Consider consulting. The question is, who do you want to consult with, and what do you want them to consult you about?

Applying Woo Strengths in Careers

These observations and suggestions will help you consider careers that could best match Woo strengths. As you think them over, select those that apply to you best.

- ☐ Choose a career in which you can constantly meet new people.
- ☐ Choose a career in which you initiate conversations and perhaps persuade people.
- ☐ Select a career that requires you to quickly form relationships and draw people to you.
- ☐ Select a career where you can deliberately build a network of people.

Chapter XI

FURTHER INSIGHTS INTO CHOOSING A CAREER

In this chapter, we will provide you with a variety of career-planning strategies. Naturally, we want you to use all of them in your career-planning process, but we hope that right now you will select at least one strategy to implement immediately.

Identify The Career Implications Of The Deepest Aspects Of Your Identity.

Ancient writers pointed to four elements that comprise the core of a person. These include heart (your deepest feelings), soul (the innermost place that contains the spark of life), mind (a variety of inner mental activities), and strength (not just physical, but all of your capabilities). Although this approach puts a slightly different twist on the concept of strengths, it offers interesting insights.

There are groups of sentence-completion statements below that reflect the deepest aspects of your personhood. Take the time to honestly and spontaneously respond to each.

Heart

1. I love _____

2. I am passionate about _____

3. I feel compassion toward _____

4. The greatest tragedy is when _____

5. I would really love to _____

Soul

1. I feel enthused when _____

2. The most meaningful thing I've ever done is _____

3. I feel a sense of destiny when _____

4. I'm inspired by _____

5. I come alive when I'm _____

Mind

1. I like to think about _____

2. I wonder why _____

3. The most important idea to me is _____

4. I value most _____

5. My deepest belief is _____

Strength

1. I am most capable of _____

2. I have a special ability to _____

3. I have a talent for _____

4. I seem gifted in the following areas: _____

5. My greatest talents are _____

What are the career implications of the deepest aspects of your identity? As you answer this question, don't look for "lightning bolt" insights. Look for patterns.

Finally, note the questions that evoke the strongest responses within you, and consider the reason why they do.

Always Have At Least One Mentor, And Always Be A Mentor To At Least One Person.

A mentor is a person you respect as being wise and someone from whom you are willing to learn. A mentor is a special type of advisor or counselor. He or she doesn't have to be "all-knowing" or a close friend, but a mentor should simply be willing and able to guide you in at least one helpful aspect. While a mentor relationship is informal, its impact can be substantial.

Please note that we suggest having at least one mentor, but more than one mentor is best because then you get additional perspectives.

In addition to having at least one mentor, you need to be a mentor to at least one other person. Without doubt, you have much to offer others. You might want to start by mentoring someone who is three or more years younger than you. Mentoring does not need to be formal. Just offer friendship to someone you care about and would like to help.

Target Your Values Before You Target A Career.

What do you value most? This is one of the first questions that you should consider in career planning.

Picture a target in your mind. It has five rings around a bull's-eye. The bull's-eye stands for the things that you value most.

Now, here is the challenge: Identify your six most important values, and then arrange them in order from the bull's-eye out, from your number-one most important value to number six.

MY VALUES TARGET

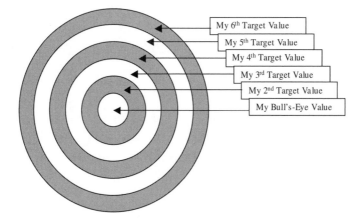

Now that you have targeted your values, remember that any career that would cause you to "miss the target" of your most important values will produce value conflicts. On the other hand, a career that helps you hit your target values produces a synergy that will likely increase your determination to achieve.

Imagine That Your Top Two Signature Themes Are Two People Who Are Planning And Deciding On A Career.

This career-planning strategy will require you to use your imagination. First, consider your top two Signature Themes. Next, imagine that these two themes are two people who totally embody the talents associated with those themes. Finally, imagine that each person is trying to decide on a career. What do you think each person would do?

Look To Your Greatest Successes For Clues To The Right Career.

The whole idea of a strengths-based approach to achieving stems from studying successful people. Extending that logic, you would be wise to study your own success patterns and then think about how your successes pertain to career planning.

To help you think about your successes, answer these three questions about your greatest triumphs:

1. What has been your most successful experience in an employment, service, or volunteer work setting?

2. What has been your most successful experience in an academic, learning, or athletic setting?

3. What has been your greatest success in an interpersonal relationship, leadership role, club, team, or organization?

After identifying your greatest success in each of those areas, focus on each success, one at a time. Relive the experience in your mind. Imagine the events and interactions surrounding your greatest successes.

As you focus on each success, ask yourself five questions.

1. What was it about that experience that makes it stand out as one of my greatest successes?

2. What did I do that contributed to producing this success?

3. What was my mental approach to this success?

4. Which talents from my Signature Themes contributed to producing this success?

5. What do I want to take from this success and make sure it is a part of my career-planning process?

Don't Plan For Your Career As If It Were Some Future Event. Begin Your Career Today And Live Accordingly.

You can begin to employ each and every one of these strategies today. You can immediately begin acting like the career professional you want to be in the future. Today, you can put forth the attitude that you know leads to success. You can begin to develop the strengths you know you will need to apply as a professional.

If you are in school, consider it your academic career. If you have a part-time or full-time job, approach your role professionally.

Do everything you can to be a person of excellence now. It is your best preparation for future excellence.

Chapter XII

BUILDING STRENGTHS-BASED RELATIONSHIPS

The benefits of the strengths approach reach beyond achievement. Here's an example. We were investigating the impact of the strengths approach on college students. Approximately 200 students in a community service class took StrengthsFinder and completed weekly exercises to help them discover and understand their talents, develop them into strengths, then apply their strengths in academics, career planning, and community service activities. At the end of the term, the students were asked what they had learned as a result of the strengths approach and how they had changed.

We expected to hear about the positive effects of strengths on achievement, and we certainly did receive that type of feedback. However, we were surprised to find that the strengths approach also generated a lot of compassion. Many reported wanting to help others discover their talents. Several wrote about trying to better understand others. Some commented about seeing people from a new perspective and how the strengths approach seemed to break stereotypes.

The fact that the strengths approach impacted so many college students in terms of their relationships surprised us at first because the course was directed toward helping students learn, achieve more effectively, and use their talents and strengths in providing community service. The improvement of interpersonal relationships was *not* a primary reason why we shared the strengths approach.

This chapter will explain how talents and strengths can be used to build relationships and how they can form a basis for fulfilling relationships.

The Basics of Fulfilling Relationships

1. **You can have a relationship with a person only to the extent that the person gives you something real to relate to.**

This may seem too elementary to mention. But have you ever tried to relate to someone and received no response whatsoever? A person (or at least a body) was present, but there wasn't anything of substance to connect with.

On the other hand, when you interact with some people, you feel a much greater sense of connection and responsiveness. You reach out with a question or a statement, and there is something real and substantial for you to connect with. These are the people with whom you have the greatest possibility for forming meaningful relationships. It is also true that people can have a relationship with you only to the extent that you provide something real about yourself for them to relate to.

2. **The experience of interpersonal closeness and intimacy is the result of people communicating their real selves.**

For intimacy to occur, people must express and listen to each other in terms of what is most real and at the core of their beings. Closeness requires more than simple communication; it requires communication on a "real-self" level.

3. **Honest commitments always enhance relationships.**

To some, open and honest communication may create an uncomfortable feeling of vulnerability. Given the discomfort and fear, we aren't likely to open up unless we know that someone is committed to us. Commitment, therefore, is a prerequisite to interpersonal closeness and intimacy.

4. **Positive relationships depend on respect.**

If you love someone, you respect him or her. Sometimes, out of desperation, we may try to fool ourselves into thinking that someone really loves us, even though we know he or she doesn't respect us. But all of our life experiences add up to the simple fact that love and respect go hand in hand.

5. **Positive relationships require action.**

When you truly care about another person, you actively seek to understand him or her, and you take action to help the person learn and grow.

Caring Is Important in Business as Well as in Friendships, Family, and Romantic Relationships.

When we talk about the importance of high-quality, caring relationships, many people think that these relationships apply only to family, friends, and people with whom we have a romantic interest. Nothing could be further from the truth. Our research clearly shows that the quality of relationships between people at work is directly related to productivity, profit, customer loyalty, and whether an employee stays with or leaves an organization. We have documented that when employees have supervisors who care about them as people, the employees are more productive, generate more profit, create greater customer engagement, and stay with the organization longer.

Awareness of Talents in Relationship Building

Just becoming aware of the fact that you have various talents can help you build healthy and productive relationships.

These relationships require not only real communication between two people, but real self-awareness. When people do not understand themselves, they tend to build false fronts and façades, and in doing so, they prevent honest communication and healthy relationships.

John Powell addresses façades in his book *Why Am I Afraid to Tell You Who I Am?* According to Powell, most people are afraid that if you really knew them, you wouldn't like them. Some people are afraid that they are empty inside or that they have no assets. Others fear that there is nothing good about them.

But all this begins to change when you become aware of the fact that you have a group of specific talents. As you become aware of your talents, and then affirm and celebrate them, there's nothing to hide. Therefore, there isn't any reason to build the façades that often destroy relationships — even though we paradoxically construct our façades to make ourselves look good enough to be loved.

Building Relationships Through Complementary Talents

During our years of strengths research, we have worked with many people who possess talents that are similar to ours, and also many whose talents were very different from ours. In both cases, the partnerships were beneficial because of the complementary nature of talents. Regardless of the similarities or differences among the talents possessed by two people, many intricate variations will exist, and, in combination, these variations will create some form of helpful interaction. While the similarities among talents can lead the two people to quickly understand and appreciate each other, the differences can result in increased effectiveness of their talents.

Imagine that Achiever is one of your Signature Themes. You would likely be the kind of person who develops a list of things to do each week and each day. Now, imagine you have a friend who complains that he or she just can't seem to get going or get things done. Think of what might happen if you were to open up and share how you, as an Achiever, set daily and weekly goals in the form of "to do" lists. If your friend were interested, you might even help him or her take some project and break it down into tasks, goals, and "to do" lists.

Reduce Conflicts by Recognizing the Talents of Others

Even when talents differ significantly, they can be complementary when the people involved respect and attempt to understand each other.

One of our most surprising findings is how frequently people come to negative conclusions because they have misperceived a person's talents. Conversely, it is amazing how rapidly differences and barriers melt away once people see each other in light of their talents.

One example involved a college board of trustees. When the trustees and their spouses took StrengthsFinder, one man discovered he had Focus and Analytical among his Signature Themes. As he talked about how his talents in those themes worked together, several board members suddenly realized that they had misunderstood this person for years.

The board members realized that when he seemed to be blocking out the rest of the group, he was actually intensely focused on the task at hand — and was very effective as a result. And when he seemed to be constantly asking questions, he wasn't just "pestering" them; he was using his Analytical talents to solve problems.

When the board members saw him in light of his talents, they realized how much he cared and they recognized the deep thought he was putting into the issues they were confronting.

Use Talents to Build Cross-Cultural Relationships

Some consider the topic of cross-cultural relationships a "hot potato" because so many sensitivities are involved. But that in itself is an excellent reason to look at these relationships from the strengths perspective. Moreover, the strengths perspective may have something important to offer in addressing the problems that run rampant among groups and cultures. The issue usually boils down to respect — respect me, respect my life experiences, and respect the culture that formed me. Recognize the fact that differences among cultures can easily lead to differences among goals, values, and ways of life.

The problem with this emphasis on *differences* is that it often generates little respect. Rather, people sometimes throw up their hands and say, in effect, "If we are that different, how can we ever build relationships with one another?"

Here's another approach. Why don't we elevate the discussion and try to focus first on where we may have things in common? Why don't we first focus on positive qualities we share? Why don't we find each other's talents, all of which are valuable and transcend cultural differences? Remember that every person, regardless of culture, nationality, or skin color, is talented in his or her own unique way and has the potential to do something truly great.

From the standpoint of building relationships, we believe that if each person assumed that every other person had the talents to do something really great, we would all interact more positively and respectfully, and this would build more positive, healthy relationships.

Chapter XIII

LET'S START A REVOLUTION

It is now time to travel into the future. Imagine what it would be like to live in a world in which we all knew and lived through our greatest areas of talent. Imagine a society in which each of us would perceive others in terms of their unique talents and strengths. What would that be like? How would people feel? How would they act? What would our social systems and organizations look like? What would happen to the relationships among cultures in a strengths-based world?

Let's begin by imagining these possibilities on a personal level. Then, let's expand our thinking to include relationships, families, the world of work, organizations, and, finally, culture.

The Impact of a Strengths Revolution on You as an Individual

To consider the impact that a strengths revolution could have on you, let's start by just imagining that you are aware of all of your greatest *areas* of talent. Knowing your Signature Themes alone is profound, but push your imagination to the point where you are aware of each and every one of your specific talents. Obviously, this tremendous level of self-knowledge would not come to you through one online assessment, through reading several books, or even through an extended series of classes. This understanding would require a lifetime of learning.

However, if you were living in a society focused on strengths, people would have been helping you become aware of your unique talents all along.

To make the image of a strengths revolution more real, imagine that by age 20 you would know each of your greatest talents and have an idea of the potential for strength they offered. You would naturally have the great self-confidence that would come with awareness of your potential, and you would likely feel humility at having been given such gifts. Awareness of your talents would also bring you a sense of identity and direction.

If you were raised in a society that rigorously helped its youth fully know and understand their talents, a lot of things would change. You would be more energized to fulfill your potential. You would be less frustrated because the trial-and-error process of discovering your talents would be greatly diminished. All in all, you would be more vibrantly alive.

The Impact of a Strengths Revolution on Relationships

If everyone were aware of their own talents and those of others, we would likely place much greater value on each other and have a new basis for forming relationships in all levels of society.

Within large or small groups, entire organizations, or even couples, two things often happen when people become aware of each other's talents. First, there is increased understanding of each other. Second, people gain greater respect for each other. Can you imagine what it would be like to live in a world where everyone understood and respected each other? Phoniness, façades, and pretense would become things of the past. Authenticity would be the new norm. And of course, with more authenticity would come greater interpersonal closeness and cooperation. This would be a tremendous benefit of a strengths revolution!

The Impact of a Strengths Revolution on Families

Starting with the most basic family unit, let's think about choosing mates. If everyone knew their own talents, and if we were able to know the talents of others, we could make better decisions when selecting a mate. We would undoubtedly want to take into consideration our areas of greater and lesser talents and then look for a mate whose talents complemented our own. We would also want our own talents to complement those of our mate.

The quality of a marriage would be better if partners knew their talents and those of their mates. This knowledge would undoubtedly result in greater cooperation. If each were working from his or her talents, they could be more effective as they worked together to reach their common goals.

If a couple really understood each other's talents, roles and responsibilities could be shaped around who they each were rather than preconceived notions about gender roles. Surely, this would reduce frustration in a marriage and increase the satisfaction that the couple would experience.

By taking the strengths perspective, individuals would feel increasingly grateful for their mates, and they would realize that together, their talents could produce at even greater levels. Their intimacy would increase as they worked together.

After the strengths revolution, married couples might have a new view of their most important roles. Wouldn't it be fantastic if husbands and wives thought that their most important responsibility was to bring out the best in their partner? Love would be expressed and experienced in the nurturing of each other's talents.

Moreover, a strengths revolution would inspire parents to identify talents in their children. And maybe this would become the new standard of parenting. Indeed, families would be much healthier if everyone knew their own talents and the talents of the other family members.

The Impact of a Strengths Revolution on the World of Work

Imagine an entire workforce made up of people who truly had the strengths to produce excellence in the roles for which they were hired. Consider what Gallup discovered in a series of surveys in 2001. Gallup investigated the extent to which the American workforce was engaged at work, and the findings were astonishing. Only 30 percent of the workers were "engaged." Fifty-four percent of the workers were not engaged, and, most distressing, 16 percent of the workforce was *actively* disengaged.

Let's consider that 16 percent. These aren't just people who don't do their work well — they actively disrupt the work of others. Companies would be better off paying them to stay home. And Gallup estimates that those actively disengaged employees cost the U.S. economy approximately $300 billion per year in lost productivity.

Why are these employees disengaged? We have great reason to believe that it is because they are not in roles that match their areas of greatest potential, that they do not have productive relationships with their managers, or that their managers are not in roles that are best suited to their talents. It is very likely that after a strengths revolution, the opposite would be true — and you would see dramatic increases in employee satisfaction, productivity, customer loyalty, and profit.

The Impact of a Strengths Revolution on Schools and Colleges

Schools and colleges typically focus on students' (a) gaining the best possible education, (b) appreciating the best in art and literature, (c) developing composition skills, (d) learning important concepts and problem-solving skills in science and mathematics, and (e) developing personal qualities that promote achievement, civility, and personal well-being. We believe that after a strengths revolution, students would achieve in each of these areas at rates higher than ever before.

Of course, after a strengths revolution, a primary emphasis would be placed on helping students become aware of their talents. We imagine one-on-one sessions, group meetings, and even workshops devoted to building this awareness throughout each person's education.

Educational planning based on strengths naturally follows from building students' awareness. This planning process would help students form goals based on their talents. Even more important, strengths-based educational planning would continuously raise the challenge of developing strengths and inventing ways of applying strengths to increase learning and improve academic performance. Finally, students would be challenged to invent ways of applying their strengths in their courses of study.

We imagine that new learning paradigms may emerge as schools and colleges become strengths-based. But the biggest change may be in the role of instructors. We can't help but ask, "What will strengths-based educators need to do?"

First, strengths-based educators would need to know their own talents and strengths. Second, they must serve as examples. Therefore, they would have to be developing and fully applying strengths as they communicate and clarify the course content in the classes they would teach. In addition, strengths-based educators would need to be able to identify the talents of students and encourage and assist the students in developing those talents into strengths. In essence, strengths-based educators would orchestrate opportunities and create activities that challenge students to apply their strengths as they learn.

The Impact of a Strengths Revolution on Society in General

We wonder about what would happen to ethnic and cultural divisions if everyone first knew each other in terms of their talents and strengths.

How would service organizations operate after a strengths revolution? What types of services would we need? This makes us wonder about which services are most important today.

How about faith-based organizations? What would happen to them, and what would their role be after a strengths revolution? How could they be a part of developing strengths? How would people be affected in terms of their faith and their view of God after everyone came to know, understand, and appreciate their talents?

We wonder about civic organizations, local and national governments, and international relations after a strengths revolution. Would we need as much government? Would we need as much policing? Would we need as many levels of bureaucracy if everyone knew and operated from their talents and strengths?

Finally, we wonder about elected officials. What if we really knew the talents and strengths of those who run for office? How many of those in office today would have been elected? Also consider the many talented individuals who, because of a strengths revolution, would choose to run for office or aspire to leadership roles after becoming aware of their abilities to serve the public at levels of excellence.

Again, we must admit we don't know the answers. But we are sure that the differences would be substantial, and we believe that they would be overwhelmingly positive.

Some Parting Thoughts

Learning about talents and developing them into strengths so that you reach your maximum potential isn't good just for you; it's good for everyone. Simply put, if we all focused our lives on making the most of our talents, the world would be a better place. And could there be an outcome more worthy than that?

Now it's time to create the future. You have your work cut out for you. Let the strengths revolution begin!

Appendix: A Technical Report on StrengthsFinder

"What research underpins StrengthsFinder, and what ongoing research is planned to refine the instrument?"

Foreword

Many technical issues must be considered in the evaluation of an instrument such as StrengthsFinder. One set of issues revolves around information technology and the expanding possibilities that Web-based applications offer for those who study human nature. Another set of issues involves what is known as psychometrics, which is the scientific study of human behavior through measurement. There are many American and international standards for psychometrics applied to test development that StrengthsFinder is required to meet (such as AERA/APA/NCME, 1999). The present report deals with some questions that emerge from those standards as well as technical questions that a leader may have about StrengthsFinder's use in his or her organization.

A few technical references have been cited for readers who wish to review primary source material. These technical materials may be found in local university libraries or on the Internet. The reader is encouraged to contact Gallup for further discussion or review the sources cited at the end of the report.

What is StrengthsFinder?

StrengthsFinder is a Web-based assessment from the perspective of Positive Psychology. There are 180 items in StrengthsFinder, presented to the user over a secure connection. Each item lists a pair of potential self-descriptors, such as "I read instructions carefully" and "I like to jump right into things." The descriptors are placed as if anchoring polar ends of a continuum. The participant is then asked to choose from the pair thestatement that best describes him or her, and also the extent to which that chosen option is descriptive. The participant is given twenty seconds to respond to a given item before the system moves on to the next item. (StrengthsFinder developmental research showed that the twenty-second limit resulted in a negligible item noncompletion rate.) The item pairs are grouped into thirty-four themes.

On what personality theory is StrengthsFinder based?

StrengthsFinder is based on a general model of Positive Psychology. It captures personal motivation (Striving), interpersonal skills (Relating), self-presentation (Impacting), and learning style (Thinking).

What is Positive Psychology?

Positive Psychology is a framework, or a paradigm, that encompasses an approach to psychology from the perspective of healthy, successful life functioning. Topics include optimism, positive emotions, spirituality, happiness, satisfaction, personal development, and well-being. These topics (and topics similar to them) may be studied at the individual level or in a work group, family, or community. While some therapists do study Positive Psychology, a typical distinction is that therapists focus on *removing* dysfunction, while positive psychologists focus on *maintaining* or *enhancing* successful function. A recent special issue of the journal *American Psychologist* (2000) gave an overview of Positive Psychology by some of its most distinguished academic researchers.

Is StrengthsFinder supposed to be a work-related inventory, a clinical inventory, both, or neither?

StrengthsFinder is an omnibus assessment based on positive psychology. Its main application has been in the work domain, but it has been used for understanding individuals in a variety of settings — employees, executive teams, students, families, and personal development. It is *not* intended for clinical assessment or diagnosis of psychiatric disorders.

Why isn't StrengthsFinder based on the "big five" factors of personality that have been well established in research journals for over twenty years?

The "big five" factors of personality are neuroticism (which reflects emotional stability — reverse-scored), extroversion (seeking the company of others), openness (interest in new experiences, ideas, and so forth), agreeableness (likeability, harmoniousness), and conscientiousness (rule abidance, discipline, integrity). A substantial amount of scientific research has demonstrated that human personality functioning can be summarized in terms of these five dimensions. This research has been conducted across cultures and languages (for example, McCrae and Costa, 1987; McCrae, Costa, Lima, et al., 1999; McCrae, Costa, Ostendorf, et al., 2000).

The major reason that StrengthsFinder is not based on the big five is that the big five is a measurement model rather than a conceptual one. It was derived from factor analysis. No theory underpinned it. It consists of the most generally agreed upon minimal number of personality factors, but conceptually it is no more correct than a model with four or six factors (Block, 1995; Hogan, Hogan, and Roberts, 1996). Some parts of StrengthsFinder could be boiled down to aspects of the big five, but nothing would be gained from doing so. In fact, reducing the respondent's StrengthsFinder assessment to five dimensions would produce less information than is produced by any current measure of the big five since those measures also report subscores in addition to the five major dimensions.

How was StrengthsFinder developed?

The conceptual basis of StrengthsFinder is grounded in over three decades of studying success across a wide variety of functions in business and education. The item pairs were selected from a database of criterion-related validity studies, including over 100 predictive validity studies (Schmidt & Rader, 1999). Factor and reliability analyses were conducted in multiple samples to assess the contribution of items to measurement of themes and the consistency and stability of theme rankings — thereby achieving the goal of a balance between maximized theme information and efficiency in instrument length.

Why does StrengthsFinder use these 180 item pairs and not others?

These pairs reflect Gallup's research over three decades of studying successful people in a systematic, structured manner. They were derived from a quantitative review of item functioning, from a content review of the representativeness of themes and items within themes, with an eye toward the construct validity of the entire assessment. Given the breadth of human performance we wish to assess, the pool of items is large and diverse. Well-known personality assessments range from 150 to upward of 400 items.

Are the StrengthsFinder items ipsatively scored, and if so, does this limit scoring of the items?

Ipsativity is a mathematical term that refers to an aspect of a data matrix, such as a set of scores. A data matrix is said to be ipsative when the sum of the scores for each respondent is a constant. More generally, ipsativity refers to a set of scores that define a person in particular but is comparable between persons only in a very limited way. For example, if you rank-ordered your favorite colors and someone else rank-ordered their favorite colors, one could not compare the *intensity* of preference for any particular color due to ipsativity; only the *ranking* could be compared. Out of 180 StrengthsFinder items, less than 30 percent are ipsatively scored. These items are distributed over the range of StrengthsFinder themes, and no one theme contains more than one item scored in a way that would produce an ipsative data matrix (Plake, 1999).

How are theme rankings calculated on StrengthsFinder?

Rankings are calculated on basis of the mean of the intensity of self-description. The respondent is given three response options for each self-description: strongly agree, agree, and neutral. A proprietary formula assigns a value to each response category. Values for items in the theme are averaged to derive a theme score. The score can be reported as a mean, as a standard score, or as a percentile.

Was modern test score theory (for example, IRT) used to develop StrengthsFinder?

StrengthsFinder was developed to capitalize on the accumulated knowledge and experience of Gallup's talent-based strengths practice. Thus, initially items were chosen based on traditional validity evidence (construct, content, criterion). This is a universally accepted method for developing assessments. Methods to apply IRT to assessments that are both heterogeneous and homogeneous are only now being explored (for example, Waller, Thompson, and Wenk, 2000). Further iterations of StrengthsFinder may well use IRT methods to refine the instrument.

What construct validity work links StrengthsFinder to measures of normal personality, abnormal personality, vocational interest, and intelligence?

StrengthsFinder is an omnibus assessment of interpersonal talents based on positive psychology. Therefore, it undoubtedly has correlational linkages to these measures to about the same extent that personality measures link to other measures in general. Convergent and discriminant validity studies are a part of past and ongoing construct validity research.

Can StrengthsFinder theme rankings change?

This is an important question for which there are both technical and conceptual answers.

Technical answers: The talents measured by StrengthsFinder are expected to demonstrate a property called reliability. Reliability has several definitions. The most important form of reliability estimate for StrengthsFinder is technically known as test-retest reliability, which is the extent to which rankings are stable over time. Almost all StrengthsFinder themes have a test-retest reliability over a six-month interval between .60 and .80; a maximum test-retest reliability score of 1 would indicate that all StrengthsFinder respondents received *exactly* the same rankings over two assessments. For respondents taking multiple administrations of StrengthsFinder, the top five themes remain exactly the same 80% of the time, and four of the top five themes remain the same 95% of the time.

Conceptual answers: While an evaluation of the full extent of this stability is, of course, an empirical question, the conceptual origins of a person's talents are also relevant. Gallup has studied the life themes of high performers in a large series of research studies combining qualitative and quantitative investigations over many years. Participants have included youths in their early teens to adults in their mid-seventies. In each of these studies the focal point was the identification of long-standing patterns of thought, feeling, and behavior associated with success. The lines of interview questioning used were both prospective and retrospective, such as "What do you want to be doing ten years from now?" and "At what age did you make your first sale?" In other words, the time frame of interest in our original studies of excellence in job performance was long term, not short term. Many of the items developed provided useful predictions of job stability, thereby suggesting that the measured attributes were of a persistent nature. Tracking studies of job performance over two- to three-year time spans added to the Gallup understanding of what it takes for a job incumbent to be consistently effective, rather than just achieving impressive short-term gains. The prominence of dimensions and items relating to motivation and to values in much of the original life themes research also informed the design of a StrengthsFinder instrument that can identify those enduring human qualities.

At this early stage in the application of StrengthsFinder, it is not yet clear how long an individual's salient features, so measured, will endure. In general, however, it is likely to be years rather than months. We may perhaps project a minimum of five years and upper ranges of thirty to forty years and longer. There is growing evidence (for example, Judge, Higgins, Thoresen, and Barrick, 1999) that some aspects of personality are predictive throughout many decades of the life span. Some StrengthsFinder themes may turn out to be more enduring than others. Cross-sectional studies of different age groups will provide the earliest insights into possible age-related changes in normative patterns of behaviors. The first explanations for apparent changes in themes, as measured, should therefore be sought in the direction of measurement error rather than as indications of a true change in the underlying trait, emotion, or cognition. The respondents themselves should also be invited to offer an explanation for any apparent discrepancies.

How can one determine that StrengthsFinder works?

Whether or not an assessment such as StrengthsFinder "works" is part of an ongoing study of the construct validity of the instrument through psychometric and conceptual review. StrengthsFinder is based on over 30 years' worth of evidence on the nature of themes and applying strengths analysis. This evidence was summarized in a recent scientific study using meta-analysis (Schmidt & Rader, 1999).

The research literature in the behavioral and social sciences includes a multitude of individual studies with apparently conflicting conclusions. Meta-analysis allows the researcher to estimate the mean correlation between variables and make corrections for artifactual sources of variation in findings across studies. As such, it provides uniquely powerful information because it controls for measurement and sampling errors and other idiosyncrasies that distort the results of individual studies. (More than one thousand meta-analyses have been published in the psychological, educational, behavioral, medical, and personnel selection fields.) For a detailed review of meta-analysis across a variety of fields, see Lipsey and Wilson (1993).

As far as StrengthsFinder is concerned, the cumulative knowledge, experience, research results, and insights that made Gallup's non-Web-based assessments so successful have been brought to bear in the Web-based StrengthsFinder; the positive psychology paradigm is the same. Client-sponsored studies have provided evidence that strengths feedback relates to various outcomes. Gallup researchers are developing publishable articles summarizing this body of knowledge.

Do StrengthsFinder scores vary according to race, sex, or age?

Gallup has studied StrengthsFinder themes in the general population. These studies aim to reflect all possible respondents in general, not applicants for or incumbents in a particular position. Score differences between major demographic groups tend to average under .04 points (i.e., four hundredths of a point) at this worldwide theme database level.

Practically speaking, these score differences are trivial. There is also no consistent pattern to the score differences. For example, one of the most important sales-related themes might be Achiever. For Achiever, males score higher than females by .031 points; nonwhite (minority group) individuals score higher than white (majority group) individuals by .048 points; and people under forty years of age score higher than those forty and over by .033 points. An important theme for managers might be Arranger. For this theme females score higher than males by .021 points; white (majority group) individuals score higher than nonwhite (minority group) individuals by .016 points; and people under forty years of age score lower than those forty and over by .053 points. Finally, many people believe that Empathy is an important theme for teaching, in particular, and human relations, in general. For this theme females score higher than males by .248 points; white (majority group) individuals score higher than nonwhite (minority group) individuals by .030 points; and people under forty score higher than those forty and over by .014 points.

Statistically speaking, with more than fifty thousand respondents in the current StrengthsFinder database, even some of these very small score differences may be deemed "statistically significant." This is simply a function of sample size. It is critical to note that the average effect size difference, expressed in units referred to as "d-prime," between men and women over all themes is .099 (that is, the average correlation between theme difference and group membership is under .05); the average d-prime effect size difference between whites and nonwhites is .133 (the average correlation equivalent is under .07); and the average d-prime effect size difference between those under forty years of age and those at least forty is .050 (the average correlation equivalent is under .03). Also, many of these small differences are favorable for what one might consider "protected" groups — nonwhites, women, and those forty or more. Finally, even significant differences do not indicate that one group has a "better" theme score than another, only that at the database level we might expect to see trends in scores for particular groups.

In reviewing these results, four conclusions seem clear to Gallup researchers. First, the average differences between theme scores for protected versus majority groups are very small, typically under .04 points, which translates to a d-prime difference score under .10. Thus, no obvious or measurement-level bias in score distributions exists between these groups. A 98-100 percent overlap exists between score distributions of comparable groups.

Second, score differences are extremely small and are only statistically significant in a few cases. This is due to the fact that more than fifty thousand respondents have completed StrengthsFinder, thus overmagnifying almost any score difference. Even when there are significant differences, the protected group is typically favored.

Third, no one theme is better than another. They simply represent the potential for different kinds of strengths. Strength building is not a zero-sum game.

In summary, trivially small differences at the worldwide database level do not translate into important practical differences at the individual level.

How can StrengthsFinder be administered, scored, and reported for individuals who are unable to use the Internet either because of disability or economic status?

In regard to economic status (a.k.a. the digital divide), possible solutions include accessing the Internet from a library or school. It should be noted that some organizations that Gallup works with do not have universal Internet access. In these cases, as with those from disadvantaged backgrounds, the solution generally has involved special access from a few central locations.

In regard to disability, a range of accommodations is available. Generally, the most effective is for the participant to turn off the timer that governs the pace of StrengthsFinder administration. Beyond this, accommodations would need to be arranged with Gallup on a case-by-case basis in advance of taking StrengthsFinder.

What is the recommended reading level for StrengthsFinder users? What alternatives are available for those who do not meet that level?

StrengthsFinder is designed for completion by those with at least an eighth- to tenth-grade reading level (that is, by most fourteen-year-olds). Trials of StrengthsFinder in our youth leadership studies have demonstrated neither significant nor consistent problems in completion of StrengthsFinder among teens. Possible alternatives or accommodations include turning off the timer feature to allow for checking a dictionary or to ask about the meaning of a word.

Is StrengthsFinder appropriate for non-English speakers?

There is overwhelming evidence from both Gallup and other research organizations that personality dimensions such as those measured by StrengthsFinder are the same across cultures. What changes is the ranking of the theme, not the nature of the theme. StrengthsFinder is currently available in 18 languages, and has been administered to over 400,000 respondents in 25 countries.

What feedback does a respondent get from StrengthsFinder?

Feedback varies depending on the reason the person completes the StrengthsFinder Profile. Sometimes the respondent receives only a report listing his or her top five themes — those in which the person received his or her highest scores. In other situations the person may also review the remaining 29 themes, along with action suggestions for each theme, in a personal feedback session with a Gallup consultant or in a supervised team-building session with their colleagues.

StrengthsFinder Technical Paper: References

The following references are provided for those readers interested in particular details of this technical report. This reference list is not meant to be exhaustive, and although many use advanced statistical techniques, the reader should not be deterred from reviewing them.

American Educational Research Association, American Psychological Association, National Council on Measurement in Education (AERA/APA/NCME). 1999. *Standards for educational and psychological testing*. Washington, D.C.: American Educational Research Association.

American Psychologist. Positive Psychology [special issue]. 2000. Washington, D.C.: American Psychological Association.

Block, J. 1995. A contrarian view of the five-factor approach to personality description. *Psychological Bulletin* 117:187–215.

Hogan, R., J. Hogan, and B. W. Roberts. 1996. Personality measurement and employment decisions: Questions and answers. *American Psychologist* 51:469–77.

Hunter, J. E., and F. L. Schmidt. 1990. *Methods of meta-analysis: Correcting error and bias in research findings.* Newbury Park, CA: Sage.

Judge, T. A., C. A. Higgins, C. J. Thoresen, and M. R. Barrick. 1999. The big five personality traits, general mental ability, and career success across the life span. *Personnel Psychology* 52:621–52.

Lipsey, M. W., and D. B. Wilson. 1993. The efficacy of psychological, educational, and behavioral treatment. *American Psychologist* 48:1181–1209.

McCrae, R. R., and P. T. Costa. 1987. Validation of the five-factor model of personality across instruments and observers. *Journal of Personality and Social Psychology* 52:81–90.

McCrae, R. R., P. T. Costa, M. P. de Lima, et al. 1999. Age differences in personality across the adult life span: Parallels in five cultures. *Developmental Psychology* 35:466–77.

McCrae, R. R., P. T. Costa, F. Ostendorf, et al. 2000. Nature over nurture: Temperament, personality, and life span development. *Journal of Personality and Social Psychology* 78:173–86.

Plake, B. 1999. *An investigation of ipsativity and multicollinearity properties of the StrengthsFinder Instrument* [technical report]. Lincoln, NE: The Gallup Organization.

References and Suggested Resources

Astin, A.W. (1977). *Four Critical Years.* San Francisco: Jossey-Bass.

Astin, A.W. (1984). Student Involvement: A Developmental Theory of Higher Education, *Journal of College Student Personnel*, 25, 297-308.

Astin, A.W. (1993). *What Matters Most in College.* San Francisco: Jossey-Bass.

Buckingham, M. & Clifton, D.O. (2000). *Now Discover Your Strengths.* New York: Free Press.

Buckingham, M. & Coffman, C. (1997). *First, Break All the Rules.* New York: Free Press.

Clifton, D.O. & Nelson, P. (1992). *Soar with Your Strengths.* New York: Dell Publishing.

Cope, R.G. & Hannah, W. (1975). *Revolving College Doors: The Causes and Consequences of Dropping Out, Stopping Out and Transferring.* New York: John Wiley & Sons.

Covey, S.R. (1990). *Seven Habits of Highly Effective People.* New York: Simon & Schuster.

Cross, P.K. (1996). New Lenses on Learning. *About Campus*, 1, 4-9.

Cushman, P. (1990). Why the Self is Empty. *American Psychologist*, 45, 599-611.

Dembo, M.H. (2000). *Motivation and Learning Strategies for College Success.* Mahwah, New Jersey: Lawrence Erlbaum.

Doby, W.C. (1997). UCLA's Academic Development Plan Response to the U.C. Outreach Taskforce Report. Unpublished manuscript, University of California at Los Angeles.

Frankl, V.E. (1959). *Man's Search for Meaning*. New York: Pocket Books.

Fromm, E. (1956). *The Art of Loving*. New York: Harper.

Greenleaf, R.K. (1977). *Servant Leadership*. New York: Paulist Press.

Harris, M.J. & Rosenthal, R. (1986). Four Factors in the Mediation of Teacher Expectancy Effects. In Robert S. Feldman (Ed.) *The Social Psychology of Education*. New York: Cambridge University Press.

Heath, R. (1967). *The Reasonable Adventurer*. Pittsburgh, PA: University of Pittsburgh Press

Jourard, S.M. (1963). *Personal Adjustment: An Approach Through the Study of Health* New York: MacMillan.

Leonard, G. (1991). *Mastery: Keys to Success and Long-Term Fulfillment*. New York: Penguin Books.

McClellan, D.C. & Steele, R.S. (1973). *Human Motivation: A Book of Readings* Moonstown, New Jersey: General Learning Press.

Pace, R.C. (1979). *Measuring Quality of Effort*. Los Angeles: UCLA Laboratory for Research on Higher Education.

Palmer, P.J. (1998). *The Courage to Teach*. San Francisco: Jossey-Bass.

Powell, J. (1970). *Why Am I Afraid to Tell You Who I Am?* Allen, Texas: Tabor Publishing.

Rosenthal, R. & Jacobson, L. (1968). *Pygmalion in the Classroom: Teacher Expectations and Pupils' Intellectual Development*. New York: Holt, Rinehart & Winston.

Senge, P.M. (1990). *The Fifth Discipline*. New York: Doubleday.

Steele, C.M. (1997). A Threat in the Air: How Stereotypes Shape Intellectual Identity and Performance, *American Psychologist*, 52, 613-629.

Stipek, D. (1998). *Motivation to Learn: From Theory to Practice*. Boston: Allyn & Bacon.

Strug, K. & Brown, G. (1996) *Heart of Gold.* Dallas, Texas: Taylor Publishing.

Tinto, V. (1987). *Leaving College.* Chicago: University of Chicago Press.

Trent, J.W. & Medsker, L.L. (1968). *Beyond High School.* San Francisco: Jossey-Bass.

Trent, J.W. (1970). The Decision to Go to College. Washington D.C.: U.S. Department of Health, Education and Welfare.

Acknowledgments

If "it takes a village" to raise a child, it could be said that it took a village or even a city to develop the StrengthsQuest program. If this work resonates with you, many people will grow from your gratitude. We will mention a few.

A broad base of people contributed to the creation of StrengthsFinder. Thousands of individuals who were judged to be successful provided interview responses from which the descriptor items were created. Hundreds of UCLA students and Gallup interviewers contributed ideas, responded to trial questions, and gave meaningful feedback.

Tom Rath, as StrengthsQuest Program Leader, along with Piotrek Juszkiewicz, the Project Manager, provided the organization, technical know-how, and inspiration to keep the entire program moving ahead day by day. Mark Pogue kept the needs of the market clearly in mind.

A gifted technical team put it all together. Jeff Briggs and Bret Bickel led a group of dedicated technologists in building the StrengthsQuest Web site. These invaluable people include: Jon Conradt, Sol Espinosa, Swapan Golla, Jeya Govindarajan, Pohl Longsine, Jesse McConnell, Christopher Purdy, Vishal Santoshi, Sam Snyder, and Collin Stork.

Editors Geoff Brewer and Paul Petters streamlined the content, with help from Kelly Henry. Drs. Maribel Cruz, Christy Hammer, Joe Streur, and Rosemary Travis, Gallup Senior Analysts, not only added insights to the text, but also checked its applicability. Dr. Phil Stone, a professor of psychology at Harvard University, and Dr. Lee Noel, founder of Noel Levitz, sharpened both the text and the goals.

Pam Ruhlman and Jules Clement have tended the collection and organization of the StrengthsFinder assessments, which have already exceeded

400,000. Thanks also go to the 40% of the 400,000, who have shared their Signature Themes with their friends.

We owe a special debt to Michael Anderson and his wife Rochelle, who solidified our determination by demonstrating the growth in confidence that came from understanding their strengths.

Irma Anderson typed the original manuscript thoughtfully and with care. Without her daily determination and enthusiasm to produce a useful book, it probably would not have happened.

Finally, we must express our gratitude for the powerful energy created by thousands of people across the country who reported great experiences after learning about their strengths, and who declared their desires to be a part of this revolutionary movement.

—Don and Chip